From Type A to Type T

How to Be a Transformational Leader in a Bottom-Line World

MARTY STANLEY

BALBOA.
PRESS

A DIVISION OF HAY HOUSE

Balboa Press books may be ordered through booksellers or by contacting:

Balboa Press
A Division of Hay House
1663 Liberty Drive
Bloomington, IN 47403
www.balboapress.com
1 (877) 407-4847

Because of the dynamic nature of the Internet, any web addresses or links contained in this book may have changed since publication and may no longer be valid. The views expressed in this work are solely those of the author and do not necessarily reflect the views of the publisher, and the publisher hereby disclaims any responsibility for them.

The author of this book does not dispense medical advice or prescribe the use of any technique as a form of treatment for physical, emotional, or medical problems without the advice of a physician, either directly or indirectly. The intent of the author is only to offer information of a general nature to help you in your quest for emotional and spiritual well-being. In the event you use any of the information in this book for yourself, which is your constitutional right, the author and the publisher assume no responsibility for your actions.

Any people depicted in stock imagery provided by Thinkstock are models, and such images are being used for illustrative purposes only. Certain stock imagery © Thinkstock.

Print information available on the last page.

ISBN: 978-1-5043-2797-8 (sc)
ISBN: 978-1-5043-2799-2 (hc)
ISBN: 978-1-5043-2798-5 (e)

Library of Congress Control Number: 2015905549

Balboa Press rev. date: 5/12/2015

I dedicate this book to the people who have the courage to lead differently, to lead boldly, to make a difference. And, it is dedicated to the people who want to be part of transforming organizations, families and communities to be in integrity, be of service and look out for the good of the whole.

This book is dedicated to people who want to Be The Change.

Table of Contents

Foreword

I met Marty several years ago and was immediately impressed with her experience and knowledge but even more impressed with the passion and commitment she has for helping individuals and organizations become their best. This is not a book about theory. Everything Marty talks about is grounded in a reality-based context. She provides specific guidance to people who are expected to solve real challenges, the most difficult and complex of which involve interactions with other people.

Marty identifies two very distinct leadership styles. Type A leaders who are typically characterized by big egos, a need to be right no matter what and the need to claim the credit when things go well. They also tend to be very self-centered and transactional, focusing more on "things" than on people. In sharp contrast, Type T leaders are typically characterized by being good listeners, supporting collaboration and focusing on accomplishing common goals for the good of the organization. In my own experience as a senior level executive, I have found that the rewards gained from what Marty defines as the Type T leadership approach are many and deeply satisfying.

Marty's depth of experience in helping Type A leaders transform to a Type T style of leadership is evident throughout this book. She provides guidance every step of the way using organizations, individual clients, her personal experiences and helpful exercises. Transforming to Type T leadership necessarily begins with acknowledging, celebrating and developing your true, authentic self.

I strongly recommend heeding her advice and doing the exercises in the book, particularly early on when the focus is on defining who you want to be and how and where you want to contribute. I found her chapters on the current multigenerational workforce especially helpful and applicable. Marty points out that there are potentially five generations of people active in the workforce today or participating within community projects. You will likely encounter multiple generations of people in your leadership role, and they all have very different characteristics, attitudes and perceptions of the world. She gives solid advice—take the time to listen to, appreciate and understand them all.

I wish Marty had written this book 10 years ago, as I could have benefited from the in-depth help it provides. I often felt isolated and was reluctant to talk about my feelings, not to mention my changing ideas about management, with my Type A colleagues. All I knew was that I could not continue down the same path for another 20 years. No more forcing myself to implement the latest corporate mandates that were in complete misalignment with my own values. The contents of this book will provide the help, support and guidance you will need to sustain your efforts as you begin, or even continue, your personal journey transforming from a Type A to Type T leader. Good luck on your own personal transformation to Type-T leadership.

Jerry Pollock—President Marketing Transitions, Kansas City, Mo. Executive Positions: Director of Marketing, Reebok International, Director, Strategic Planning, Reebok International; VP Marketing, St. Louis, Music

Acknowledgments

Where to begin? I am so grateful to so many people who have had a profound impact during the course of writing this book.

It is a compilation of experiences and lessons learned during my years in the corporate world and as a solo entrepreneur.

Starting my career as an aspiring leader, I am indebted to the founders and leaders of a company, Employers Health Insurance, now Humana, that gave me incredible and invaluable experiences that provided the foundation for the career I have today. I am grateful for all of the people who helped me build and transform the human resource departments at three amazing companies and learn the importance of organizational culture, leadership and the impact on the bottom line.

As a solo-entrepreneur for over 15 years, I am truly grateful for the trust and confidence that my clients have placed in me as they embarked on their journeys to higher levels of leadership. It is through them that I have learned what Type T leadership is, how it works and why it's important. They have taught me the transformational leadership skills and attitudes that are essential, not only now and for the future success of any organization, but for our own health, the health of our families and our communities.

And there are individuals who have made huge contributions in formulating the Type T concept. I was introduced to Janet O. Hagberg's book *Real Power: Personal Power in Organizations* over 20 years ago, and it had a profound impact on my understanding of stages of leadership. Her insights provided a perspective that contributed to the Type T concept.

Another person who was essential to the "birthing" of this book is Mindy Gibbins-Klein, president of The Book Midwife, who encouraged me to participate in her program "Writing a Book in 90 Days." This was the catalyst that propelled me to finally write my second book. She provided the structure and process that drew from my depths the message I wanted to tell, but didn't know it and didn't know how to tell it. And my trial "readers"—the people who previewed the book after it was written in 90 days and provided the feedback that I needed to keep going! Jacqueline Chanda, Linda Claycomb, John Escalada, Barb Larson, Cathy Griggs Newton, Jerry Pollack, Susan Rustici, Nathan Soltice and Candy Whirley. Thank you for taking the time to read my draft and provide the loving and caring suggestions for making it better.

Special thanks go to my mastermind buddies, Cathy Griggs Newton and Candy Whirley, for understanding when I hit writers' roadblocks, barriers and resistance. They provided encouragement, support and resources, especially in the form of recommending an extraordinary editor, Max Garrison.

Max has been the person who helped put structure to what seemed to be rambling thoughts and stories. She did what I needed most, which was to ask the questions and probe the nuances of the murky world of corporate culture and have me explain better what the readers want to know about how to be a transformational leader in a bottom-line world. And most importantly, through what seemed to me to be annoying questioning and irritating persistence, we arrived at a title and consistent message that makes my heart sing! She was consistently encouraging about the content and the process, and I am truly grateful for her contribution.

And finally, I am grateful to Balboa Press for the opportunity to work with them in publishing this book. To be part of a Hay House Publishing family is indeed an honor and privilege.

Introduction

If you believe that organizations can't change unless the people leading, managing, and doing the work change too, this is the book for you. Successful organizational leaders must know how to navigate personal change and transformation before they can, in turn, transform the organizations and the people they lead.

From Type A to Type T: How to Be a Transformational Leader in a Bottom-Line World is designed to guide you on your personal journey of finding your authentic self, so you can then lead changes that are balanced with integrity, authenticity and well-being in the workplace, in organizations and in communities.

The source for all of it is your personal life.

It's about the journey we are on as continuously evolving individuals and leaders. If you, like me, climbed the ladder, accomplished your goals and still felt like something was missing, I hear you and can tell you it's not your imagination. Trust me when I say you're not alone. And, consider the concept that you may have been living other people's dreams or aspirations. So many times we make choices based on our parents' or spouse's expectations, what's best for children or family or, truth be told, sometimes to keep up with the "Joneses."

It's not too late—it's never too late— to live and lead in an authentic manner, one that emphasizes empowerment and collaborative communication with the people at work and in our lives. It's been proven that healthy, collaborative and empowered business cultures not only fit the new, fast-changing world we live in, but are more productive and profitable. Have you yearned to work in this kind of environment? Have you wanted to be a part of leading this kind of movement? Are you ready to transform yourself and your workplace? If so, know that I am ready to help you with the discovery and application of transformational leadership.

Allow me to start by briefly sharing my story because for as long as I can remember, I have transformed and reinvented my life, personally and professionally. However, the shift from corporate management to solo entrepreneur, from playing the "corporate game" to discovering and being in integrity with my true self is the reason and impetus for writing this book. It's the "been there, done that" experience that will best connect us and enable me to successfully help you transition and transform personally and professionally.

The stage of my journey now, as a national speaker, consultant and executive coach is part of a long and winding road that began in corporate management. Yet, despite the particular challenges of each position, there was a common theme: I was required to help each organization change in some way.

Early on in my career, I was hired to create and implement almost all of the human resource processes for a fast-growing, entrepreneurial company in Green Bay, Wisconsin. I designed and implemented everything from compensation and benefit systems to employee relations, performance management, training and development and corporate wellness. During my tenure, the company grew from 250 employees to over 1700 and became a nationwide, billion-dollar company, recognized for their innovative approach to training and development and designated as one of the top 25 corporate wellness programs in the country. There were three buy-outs before I left, and the company is now owned by Humana.

The next corporate stop was Blue Cross Blue Shield of Kansas City, Missouri, where I had been hired to basically make the same changes but in a smaller, very traditional company that had lost market share primarily (and ironically) by losing business to my former company in Green Bay. They needed to change attitudes and approaches to meet the changing needs of their customers and the marketplace. This was more about cultural change and getting people aligned with the strategic direction. There were new challenges, and I was still happy and climbing the leadership ladder with increasing responsibilities, impressive titles and perks and more money.

The final stop on my corporate travels, before I became an entrepreneur, was vice president of human resources for AMC Entertainment. Believe me! The movie industry was way more fun than insurance! Once again, I was hired to help an organization with significant change. Their new strategic direction would require hiring over 500 managers and 2000 new staff employees to run megaplexes. Dramatically different skills were required to manage the megaplexes than the smaller units that were the norm at that time. Again, all human resource processes had to be revamped to meet corporate objectives and align to the strategic direction. How we hired, trained, compensated and rewarded people would be very different, based on the new business model. It was great fun and challenging to create the right structures and processes to fit this new environment and hire the best people for a challenging job in the hospitality/entertainment industry.

Let me just say that, based on these experiences, I understand the challenges of creating a vision and implementing the steps to make it happen. I understand the process of change, creating an organizational culture that is aligned with strategic goals and what can happen when it all comes together (or not!).

These experiences exposed me to diverse areas and approaches needed not only for organizational change, but personal transformation as well. I was learning and seeing first-hand that the culture and success of a business depends on the people involved, and this connection and interdependence was getting significantly clearer. No doubt you've experienced this in your own profession; employees are the foundation and the strength of the business depends on them.

At some point, I realized that I had reached the peak of my corporate career in terms of title, status, influence, money. This realization brought good news and bad news. The good news was that I'd had a good run in the corporate world, worked for terrific companies and was able to successfully implement the new processes and structures that empowered employees and contributed to organizational success. The bad news? I was discontented, disillusioned. I had been in positions I thought could make the difference for people at all levels in an organization, and yet I felt stuck. There was only so much I could do. How could this be? I had everything I had wanted and worked for! How could I be unhappy? It's hard to put into words. Somehow, all of these outward successes weren't enough. I wanted more, but not in a material sense. I wanted a bigger purpose, peace of mind, full self-expression in a creative sense and contribution in a broader scope. Living and working in a bottom-line, linear world made this very difficult. I felt confined and restricted. And I knew I wanted to reach a broader audience, impact more people and work with diverse organizations. This could only happen if I ventured out on my own.

So, I left the corporate world after 20+ years of progressive and exciting experiences to be an entrepreneur and "help people." I became certified as a life coach and then a business coach, at a time when people said, "Can you make money doing that?" The simple answer was, *yes*. There was, and still is, a need for an independent, objective approach to change, whether it's for personal, professional or organizational purposes. While my business has morphed and changed since I started on my own in 2000, the essence has remained the same. I've survived three recessions, perhaps because of my ability to adapt to change rapidly, but I believe it's because of my guiding principles: to *empower* people with knowledge, skills, tools, resources and abilities, so change can be *regenerating and sustainable.*

This philosophy has served me well. Because the world was turned upside down in 2008 and there have been so many changes, organizations that have stayed the same have become irrelevant. The traditional styles of management (which I refer to as Type A leadership) and conventional business models aren't as profitable, acceptable or desired in this new economy. Rapidly changing business conditions, technology, legislation, societal norms and shifting demographics are the new normal, and organizations and their leaders will need to adapt and modify to be competitive.

Before I delve into how transformational leadership fits into all of this, let me share the significant characteristics of those I call Type T leaders. These leaders exhibit the traits of authentic leadership. They are people who lead from the inside out—using their intuition and true sense of self, creating an authentic style. Focused on collaboration and the well-being of every stakeholder in the organization, from entry level to management, with vendors and suppliers, they lead with integrity, accountability and consistency.

A shift from Type A to Type T is needed now more than ever. Leaders need to transform how they lead to a more accountable, collaborative, holistic and empowering leadership model. Are you ready to be a transformational leader?

How to Use this Book

From Type A to Type T: How to Be a Transformational Leader in a Bottom-Line World is set up in five interrelated and progressive sections. The first one provides a foundation for being a Type T leader. It provides an explanation of traditional and emerging leadership styles, the relevance and benefit of alignment and accountability in your personal life, as well as how to achieve and apply it. The following four sections take this base of knowledge and transformative thinking and apply it to you as a business leader from what it "looks like" to action steps. Entities will be referred to as "organizations" or "businesses", as the skills and mindset cross over to not-for-profits and associations regardless of size or purpose. The end result is to create healthy, profitable, empowered and productive employees and successful organizations.

Throughout the book, I share not only my experiences in the process, but also some examples and stories from clients and organizations

I have worked with over the years. While the names of individuals have been changed, you may be able to relate to this person or their experiences. As you read these, think about yourself and your company or your communities. How do the concepts apply? The more you can relate to the examples or stories, the more helpful it will be for you.

There will be some suggested exercises, and I encourage you to do them, as they will deepen your understanding and help you facilitate your changes. These exercises are located in the Appendix by chapter number and title. This book is meant to be a time for reflection and focus for the future. Take advantage of the opportunity to think about who you are, your impact and influence. And then, take the time to be deliberate and intentional about creating your future for the next stage of your life.

But, most importantly, use this book as an opportunity to acknowledge yourself and all that you have done to get you where you are today and to joyfully create the next stage in your life. Welcome—you are not on this journey alone.

Type T Leadership:
The Journey Begins at Home

Chapter 1

You're Not Crazy

She sat staring at me, eyes filled with tears. "I never cry. I don't know why I'm crying now."

And so it began. Barbara hated her job of 20 years. As an officer of the company, she led a team of over 100 people. She didn't want to come to work anymore. She couldn't relate to her colleagues. She wasn't happy.

"Am I crazy? I make really good money. I have a great husband. I'm successful beyond my wildest dreams. Why am I so unhappy? People would give anything to have my life. What's wrong with me?"

Nothing.

Over the years, I have heard this scenario hundreds of times. It usually occurs for women in their late 40's and 50's. For men, it is usually a little later in life, maybe 55-65. However, I have had two male clients in their late 40's who expressed similar feelings—both business owners. They described their lives as being "flat-lined."

That's the general feeling for these people who would typically describe themselves as raging Type A personalities. Briefly stated for background purposes, people who are Type A are competitive, achievement oriented, aggressive and, very often, workaholics. It would not be uncommon for Type A's to be task-oriented, concerned with efficiency and struggle with collaboration. They also like to be in the spotlight and often are, as they can be highly successful in their endeavors.

So, naturally, this deadened feeling is very disconcerting. For most of these people, it's usually a result of having achieved a high level of success and once arriving at the top—whatever the "top" is for them—they find themselves looking out and thinking: "This is it?"

"I've worked all these years, sacrificed friends and family and put my career ahead of many things. Now I'm in a position of influence and "power," and it doesn't seem to be that great. What's wrong with me?"

As I see it, it's part of the leadership process of being more discerning. It's a stage where real leaders are discovering a higher purpose for their leadership.

Janet Hagberg's Stages of Power

There is some interesting research to support this shift in how people approach leadership. According to Janet O. Hagberg, author of *Real Power—Stages of Personal Power in Organizations*, people demonstrate different levels of power. While there are "6 Stages of Power," in most organizations, one will usually find people who are at Stages 2, 3 and 4.

At Stage 2, people are either entering their professional career and learning the ropes or are dependent upon their supervisor for information and approval to take action. They have gone from Stage 1 of being secure but feeling powerless and trapped to power by association.

While these first two stages of power are necessary steps in the process, for our purposes, we are going to focus on Stage 3, specifically the similarities between Type A personality traits and those identified in Hagberg's Stage 3. When we talk about leaders in an organization, Stage 3 is the norm. The commonalities between Stage 3 and Type A are egocentricity, competitiveness, ambition, power through knowledge and expertise, a rational perspective and a need for control. This type of leadership is very bottom line oriented. If you can't show the benefit to bottom line profitability, the Type A leader may ignore or disregard ideas as "fluff."

It's also important to take a brief look at the idea of power and its ramifications, which is common in organizations. The Stage 3 or Type A style of leadership is a very masculine style, as evidenced by bravado and competitiveness, being the expert and a high desire for all the perks and status to prove you've "made it."

Many of the symbols that "prove you've made it" are wearing a trendy, expensive watch, designer shoes, the luxury car or club memberships. I remember meeting a young "up and comer" who ordered a very expensive scotch on the rocks, and he secretly confided to me that it was part of his desire to be viewed as more mature and successful.

When women are in this stage of power, they adapt more masculine language, maybe even style of dress. To succeed, they've been told to "toughen up." Back in the 1980's, as women were rising in the ranks of corporate leadership, almost every woman read John Malloy's *Dress For Success* and started sporting boxy suits and perky bow ties, so they could look the part.

Today, fortunately, women have given up the manly clothes but are still cautioned not to look too feminine and God forbid—don't cry. To succeed in today's corporate environment, women have to prove themselves by being tough, rational, non-emotional, results oriented.

While those are not bad qualities, women inherently have additional skill sets that aren't necessarily valued in Stage 3 organizations or leadership teams. And because for the past 40 years most organizations have been male dominated, women have learned to adopt or emulate many masculine characteristics in the workplace.

Some women have learned those skills all too well—perhaps to an extreme. I had a client who was an officer at a large financial institution. I was hired as an executive coach because Jean had been promoted many times and was now at a senior level, when her boss basically said, "Stop acting that way. You're too aggressive." When I met her, she told me in a very defiant way, "I'm the one they go to, to get the job done!" I could only imagine all the dead bodies left in the wake of her steamroller approach.

This was a classic Stage 3 woman. Aggression in women is not a valued trait in the organizational leadership ranks. Assertiveness is more acceptable, but women can't be too conciliatory either. Successful women in organizations learn how to survive in this kind of culture. At least until the day they begin to feel like they've lost themselves and are asking, "What happened to me?" They begin to feel like an impostor and really uncomfortable with who they are or how they feel they are projecting themselves.

For most men, "Stage 3" isn't a "stage" but just who they are naturally in organizations, more competitive, goal focused, bottom line oriented, analytical and rational. It's not personal—it's business.

Enter Stage 4

Yay! Hagberg says that Stage 4 is the first real stage of leadership because it's at this stage that there is an integration of the traditional feminine qualities of reflection, competence without bravado and mentoring. Leaders at this stage are less egocentric and are more concerned about long-term impact and development of people.

Once men, and women especially, get past the thought that they're not crazy for not wanting all the status and outward glory, they can start developing deeper connections and contributing to the big picture initiatives in their organizations. They slide in easily to this level of leadership—provided their organization respects and honors this approach. Not all do.

For both, transitioning to leadership at the Stage 4 level of power is very uncomfortable. Generally, it's at this point that men and women feel like they have "lost their edge," with men thinking they're going "soft." It's particularly hard for men at this point because the expectations are so hard-wired for them to be more aggressive, more analytical, more bottom line oriented. When men start to question themselves and a greater purpose, it's often unspoken, dismissed and suppressed. Ideas or initiatives that benefitted employees or customers, that in the past were disregarded because they didn't show a direct benefit to the bottom line, may now seem like a good idea—because it's the "right" thing to do.

We have been conditioned to believe that the Stage 3 power of leadership is the be all and end all. Most advertising and media target people at this level. It's the American dream. According to Hagberg, people experience a "crisis" which will precede moving to the next stage of power. The crisis can be personal or professional, but it's like a wake-up call that sends an alarm saying, "You can't continue like this." So, naturally, when a leader experiences the crisis before moving to Stage 4, it is often overwhelming.

Many times, the "crisis" takes the form of a major loss, such as a loss of a parent, spouse or close friend. In Barbara's case, within a 15-month period, her father, who was her role model and confidant, had died. Her kids had gone to college, and she and her husband were empty nesters and learning to get to know each other again. And the dog died. Not surprisingly, it was the loss of the dog that put her over the edge.

She felt like a fish out of water. In fact, having gone through this experience myself, I remember it as feeling like I was a snake shedding its skin.

When a snake sheds its skin, it rubs up against something sharp to help the process of releasing the old skin. Slowly, the snake rubs against a sharp object, slowly slithering out of the dead skin—only to have the raw sensitive skin exposed to the air, while still dragging the dead skin behind, until the process is complete. Gradually the new skin becomes more supple, and the snake can move freely again.

Transformational Leadership

Transformational leadership requires personal change as well—in order to find your true, authentic self, which is where the transformational journey begins. It's uncomfortable to start and, like the snake shedding its skin, we can feel like we're rubbing up against sharp objects. Perhaps we're experiencing resistance to some of our new ideas and suggestions. Or maybe our reactions to people and situations have shifted, and people are uncomfortable with our new approach. Maybe the sharp objects we're rubbing up against are our bosses and organizational practices that seem incongruent to our new direction. During this transition time, we're still raw, experimenting and practicing and then testing our new directions and ideas. Yet, we are still in the old environment and must carry around what seems like the dead weight of the old ways of being until the transition is complete.

During this time, it's like we're hanging on a great divide—not ready to take the leap to the other side but trusting that the net will be there if we fall. And we trust that when we do take the leap, there will be others ready to catch us and welcome us to the big picture of leadership.

And the big picture of leadership requires a transformational shift from Type A to Type T leadership. Just remember—you're not crazy because you no longer can, or want to, be a Type A leader. You're on the path to discovering the higher purpose for your leadership. As you transition to the new model of transformational leadership, you will feel alive, vibrant and happy. People will follow the new you. It's an exciting time. And just remember, it takes courage to cross the divide from traditional, egocentric leadership to true, authentic leadership.

Trust the process and know that you're ready to be Type T!

Let's get started!

Chapter 2

Foundational Tools for Transformation

As you embark on your quest for discovery of your higher purpose and more authentic leadership, know that to do so is a step in the direction of improved mental, physical and spiritual health. Perhaps this sounds odd, but consider the impact of the lack of alignment when you feel that who you are is no longer in sync with the person you knew yourself to be.

For years, you probably saw yourself as the hard-driving, Type A, results-oriented leader. Then, with what seemed like a sudden jolt, you felt like you could no longer operate that way. Now, you feel compelled to be more inclusive, more nurturing and sensitive to other people's ideas, situations and feelings. You start to trust your intuition more, and it feels awkward, yet compelling. As you trust your intuition, your responses and choice of words in responding to people seem different but more authentic than ever before. Internally, the voice in your head is saying: How did I think to say that? Where did that come from? That was really great!

First of all, know that this is normal.

Know that you are being drawn to a healthier style of leadership because you are speaking from your heart, not your head. The authentic you is emerging, and it feels good.

The best way to adapt to this shift in integrating your head and your heart is to understand the impact of your thoughts, words and actions on your overall health and well-being. According to scientific studies, your thoughts are vibrational energy because everything is constantly in motion, your thoughts can gain momentum! If you hold a thought for 17 seconds or more, whatever is on that frequency will come back to you. Basically, positive thought energy will attract positive things. Every thought you have has an impact on you, and these thoughts affect your perspective and your subsequent actions. It only makes sense that positive thought energy will attract positive things.

Consider the expressions "birds of a feather flock together" or "likes attract likes." Imagine that your thoughts are like a giant magnet, and whatever you're thinking about, for 17 seconds or more, will be reflected in your life.

I invite you to consider what I call Red Light Days and Green Light Days.

Here's how it works: You wake up, and you think, "Oh, I am so tired today. I don't want to go to work, I just can't deal with all the complaining clients and difficult co-workers . . ." Then you drive to work and hit every red light. You get a crummy parking space (in the rain, of course), and when you get to your office, someone tells you two people are out sick. Mid-day, someone asks you, "How's your day going?" to which you respond, "It's started out bad, and it's gone downhill since then. " This is definitely a Red Light Day.

Guess what? I hate to tell you this, but you're just getting more of what's on your vibrational frequency. You started out the day focused on not wanting to go to work and deal with difficult people. And with each event after that, the red lights, the parking space, the people being absent from work, you're focused on the negative aspects and all of the same crummy things accumulating, adding to your perception that it's a bad day. In fact, you're merely unconsciously reinforcing that perspective each time you think about how things are going downhill and attracting more of the same. Your negative thoughts gained momentum.

Let's see what happens with a different perspective: You wake up and think "WOW! I must have had a fabulous dream—I can't wait to get to work." You breeze through every green light, you get rock-star parking, and when you walk inside the building, people say "You look Mahhhvelous!" People are returning phone calls, and you're getting all the information you need to complete a project easily and effortlessly. And then, mid-day, a co-worker says, "I'm all caught up with my work; can I help you out today?" This is definitely a Green Light Day!

And it seems that the rest of the day is great. Even if there is a glitch, it's not overwhelming, like on the red light days. The kind of thinking that happens on red light days wears you down—emotionally, physically and mentally. At the end of the day, you'll go home feeling exhausted and like you didn't get anything done.

The green light days, however, are uplifting, productive and fun! You go home at the end of the day feeling energized, happy and alive. You are able to engage with your friends and family and feel more motivated to tackle a project at home or even go for a walk, exercise or get together with friends. You may be wishing that every day could be a green light day. And they can. Because from this point forward, you get to choose, on a moment-by-moment basis, what kind of day you're going to have.

Yes, that's right. You get to choose. In the past, you probably thought you just had to deal with whatever negative circumstance or situation you encountered. Some people may think they are victims of fate or they have a black cloud over their head. It doesn't have to be that way. That person doesn't have to be you.

Keep in mind that what you focus on is what you get. So, if you're focused on doom and gloom, that's what you'll get! And if you're focused on people collaborating or things going smoothly, you'll experience more of that. You choose whether the red lights are annoying and irritating or if they are a chance to observe your surroundings, hear the music on the radio or take a deep breath and enjoy the slower pace. The "crummy parking space" may be an opportunity to get a little exercise or have a good laugh at yourself when you see your wet hair because you forgot your umbrella.

When you change your outlook, you alter your outcomes. You can alter your perspective at any given point, if you choose.

So the key is to recognize when you're on the downward spiral of negativity and stop it as fast as you can. Because, again, if you hold a thought for 17 seconds or more, whatever is on that emotional frequency will continue.

To help you grasp the importance of managing your thoughts and emotions, I read some amazing research that illustrates the importance of the connection of body, mind and spirit that I'd like to share with you. There was a 30-year study done at the Institute of Advanced Theoretical Research in Arizona that measured the impact of emotions on the body. In short, they found that if people hold negative emotions for long periods of time, those emotions will wear the body down and can eventually impact a person's immune system, potentially causing illness. Some of the negative emotions included anger, fear, apathy, guilt, hate, blame and despair. Conversely, when people experienced positive emotions for longer periods of time, they tended to be healthier, have stronger immune systems and fewer illnesses.

The positive emotions included love, joy, serenity, forgiveness, trust and acceptance.

If we go back to the concept that whatever you think about and whatever you focus on for 17 seconds or more will come back to you, it's even more important now to manage what you think about, how long you think about it and the emotion you have around that thought. Because, as you can now see, your thoughts can impact your health.

On those days when you go home exhausted and think that you really didn't accomplish very much, there's a good chance that you spent a lot of time "in your head," obsessing about the past or something that went wrong. These repetitive thoughts or scenarios that you play over and over in your head can be like a broken record. Many times it's the same scenario about something that happened a week, a year or a decade ago. The scenarios are usually the same, and you continue to re-enact them—over and over and over. Just know that this is not problem solving because the outcome is always the same. By repeatedly reliving these experiences in your head, you are unconsciously wearing yourself down, emotionally and physically.

One way to guard against this is to do what I call, "The Two Week Challenge." The way the challenge works is to listen to your thoughts and the words that you speak for two full weeks. Observe how frequently you obsessively think about something in the past that, in reality, can't ever change. Listen to how many times you tell the same sad story about how somebody disappointed you or you didn't get what you wanted. It can sound a lot like a country western song where someone did you wrong. During The Two Week Challenge, when you notice this repetitive negative thinking, STOP IT as fast as you can. Because, as you now know, if you hold a thought for 17 seconds or more, you'll just experience more of those depressing emotions or experiences. Also, when you take The Two Week Challenge, notice if your thoughts and words are aligned with what you really want or if you are talking about things that aren't important to you or in line with your current direction in life. Your thoughts and language serve as a precursor of things to come! Manage your thoughts wisely.

Shedding, Grieving, Letting Go

One thing to keep in mind in the early stages of this transition to Type T leadership is that you are testing and trying out new ways of thinking that are more intentional and deliberate than ever before. You are aligning your thoughts, words and actions for the future. In some ways, you will be giving up a piece of your old self and old patterns that can no longer support you as you move forward. It's important to recognize that all that you have done in the past has gotten you to where you are today. Honor that past and appreciate it, while at the same time understand that what worked for you before may not serve you in the future.

It can be hard to let go of the past, old behaviors or traditional ways of thinking about things. Allow yourself time to grieve. For many hard-driving Type A's, it's difficult to let their guard down and acknowledge a level of sadness or fear as to what the future might hold. It's ok to cry, if that's what happens when you allow yourself to feel the waves of uncertainty that come with this kind of transformation. As the tearful Barbara from Chapter One said, "I never cry! My dad would be horrified if he knew I cried about this. And my boss would walk away if I cried in front of him. I feel so weak! I hate it."

Welcome to the world of experiencing all the feelings and emotions that have been bottled up for years. Many successful leaders were raised to believe that they had to slog through and keep a stiff upper lip and deny the existence of any sadness or disappointment. It doesn't have to be that way. In fact, part of being a Type T leader is a willingness to gradually let down the guard, be more open to life and be somewhat vulnerable.

In Barbara's situation, her tears were an accumulation of all the losses she'd experienced—her dad's death, her children going to college, getting married and now being an empty nester and the sudden loss of a beloved pet. My advice to her was to find a place of solitude and "Wail Away! Let 'er rip!"

Mourning the loss, be it a cumulative set of losses like Barbara's or the loss of your "old self" and making way for the new, deserves a rite of passage.

When giving up your old self and paving the way for the new you, several things can happen. It's important to acknowledge that the skills and behaviors that got you to where you are today, most likely won't be the skills and behaviors that will take you to the next level of your higher purpose and authentic leadership.

First, you may find that you are changing some of your assumptions or some long-standing beliefs you had about yourself. For example, one client, Martin, was a successful CPA and a financial planner. While he was very skilled at working with numbers and doing financial analyses to help his clients, he sheepishly admitted that he no longer enjoyed working with numbers. As we started exploring other career options, Martin stated that every career assessment he'd taken said he should be a hospital administrator. And as he said, "But I HATE hospitals!"

What he did discover, in the process and at the age of 55, was that he wanted to become a minister. After transitioning his business and finishing his studies at the seminary, he is now a chaplain at—you guessed it—a hospital! And loving every minute of it.

As people begin to transform and align their higher purpose and practice authentic leadership, not only do they often change jobs or careers, but, frequently, they change their physical appearance, as they allow their more authentic self to emerge at this point in life. For example, one of my clients, Susan, was an executive director for a trade association. She used to dress in fairly masculine clothes and sensible shoes. Her short-cropped hair and no makeup meant no nonsense to her members, who happened to be mostly men. She had kind of a dowdy, Birkenstock appearance that served her well when she started in her position. As her members listened to her pragmatic approach, she built credibility. But, as the organization and her self-confidence in her role grew, the association broadened to a much bigger arena of influence in the city. The granola image no longer served her, and she blossomed into a stunning, sophisticated 60+ woman in stilettos and contemporary and trendy business attire that suited her new role and savoir-faire. Her cropped hair was restyled to a casually spiked look, and she started wearing subtle makeup, which brought out her lovely, mature features that instilled confidence in her ability and influence to get things done in a whole new way. Not only did her organization become nationally known, she doubled her income too!

I too, watched not only my appearance, but also my home transform, as I became more comfortable with this emerging, powerful and authentic stage of leadership. As a vice president of human resources for several large and international organizations, I felt I had a role to play and had to look and live the part of a corporate executive. I had a very large and lovely, fairly formal home in a prestigious part of town. It suited me just fine because, due to travel, late nights working and attending community events, I was rarely there. When I left the corporate world and began my consulting practice, I had a home-based business. This was a huge change, as I was home almost all the time now. And the more time I spent at home, the more unlivable the house seemed. Being an older, spacious home, it was "demanding," constantly needing attention, repairs and upkeep. The furniture, which seemed great when doing business entertaining, now seemed stiff and uncomfortable. The colors and lighting felt cold and impersonal. In many ways, I've thought of this house as a reflection of who I was in the corporate world.

As I was establishing my new purpose and calling in life, the structure and furnishings of the house seemed painfully opposite to the person I was becoming. I painted and repainted, sold furniture, bought new furniture. I changed as much as I could to "warm it up" and eventually moved to a smaller house—one that could fit on the first floor of the old one! The new house exuded warmth and welcome to all who entered. I was at peace. The structure, environment and furnishings were a better reflection of my emerging style and approach, which could never have happened in my previous home.

So, when you are emerging to the next stage of authentic leadership, not only do your thoughts and words need to be aligned, but you just might find that your appearance and lifestyle may need some alignment as well to create more congruency to who you are. The emergence of the "inside" you will have positive and, possibly surprising, ramifications.

Friends and Family

When you spend years in a particular kind of environment, adapting and molding yourself to fit in and shaping yourself to meet that culture's style, it can be hard to break free. Keep in mind that over the course of your career, you were growing and learning and doing the best you could with the knowledge, tools and resources you had available at the time. As your career was progressing, you were becoming less dependent on your supervisors and beginning to establish your own credibility. Then you hit your stride in being the expert and basking in all the glories of success. Since Type A leadership has been the traditionally accepted way to lead and communicate, other styles may be considered odd or out of place, sometimes even unacceptable, depending on the organizational culture. The peak of being a Type A can be a pretty heady experience and one that is hard to give up. This is just part of the process of "shedding the old skin" and feeling a little raw.

In the early stages of your personal and professional transformation, friends and family may wonder what's going on with you. This is a particularly sensitive time because there will be people in this group, family included, who may question your thinking and even your sanity. Be a little cautious about how much you share and to whom in these early stages. When you are going through a major transformation such as this, many people will have a hard time distinguishing that this is *your* experience and *your* path, not theirs. Many will internalize your words and start to question themselves. For example, have you ever had the experience of questioning your own marriage or committed relationship when you hear that friends are divorcing? "But they seemed so happy! Maybe I'm not seeing everything in my relationship . . ." Remember that they are not thinking about you but, instead, thinking about themselves and responding to you through their own filters.

This is a very personal time when you are examining your higher purpose of leadership and transforming to your authentic self. It's your time to explore personal goals and discover the best direction in life that will bring more satisfaction and feelings of contribution and alignment. This is not the time to try to convince others of your plans and ideas or to try to get them to listen to you, unless they are supportive of your exploration and sincerely inquire about your future direction. Move on. Or if that's not an option for you, minimize the time or topics discussed with them. Being with resistant family members or long-time friends can be the hardest because they liked or were comfortable with "the old you." Don't try to convince them or explain yourself. They'll just find it annoying and confusing. Instead, find topics that are common ground.

Others will be excited for you or at least be interested in listening, and quietly supporting you. Hang out with these people. You don't need to be around naysayers or people who think you're crazy. At this point, you have already questioned yourself and are moving on to explore directions that are more congruent with what rings true for you. You don't necessarily need to be around people who are second-guessing your judgment, unless they are providing loving and supportive guidance that is in *your* best interest, not theirs.

It may be time to find new groups or seek out like-minded people. In subsequent chapters, we'll be focusing on creating the intentions for what you want during this transition time and for a future that will lead to more personal fulfillment and a higher level of leadership in your career. You will find that as you create clear and powerful intentions, you will be attracting more of what you want—including people, resources and information that support your new vision.

In the meantime, it may be appropriate to grieve relationships that are ending or grieve the realization that a friendship may not be there going forward. One woman wept openly as she described the realization that a long-time, childhood friend, who was also a coworker, was openly backstabbing her for the leadership decisions she was making that were in the best interest of the organization. And, she was realizing that the person might not have been a true friend for the long term. It hurt.

People may be in our life for a reason, a season or even a life-time. Take some time to think about those who are or have been in your life and those who may go with you on your journey of self-exploration.

If and when you identify people who may have been in your life for a reason or season that is no longer relevant, it still hurts and it's ok to be sad. Learn from it and focus on what you know is right for you now. Hopefully you can take comfort in knowing that this is simply one part of the process of transforming from the inside out.

Chapter 3

Transformation From the Inside Out

People who have shifted their leadership styles have acknowledged that the process of transformation can be exhausting. Having also experienced this myself, new nourishment will be needed to sustain you and build up your Type T leadership "muscles." During this time you will want to pay extra attention to your body, mind and spirit.

When it comes to caring for their body, mind and spirit, there's often a difference between how Type A's and Type T's approach it. Type A's will latch on to the next big trend in food, exercise or relaxation because it's the "in" thing to do. They are somewhat competitive about it and want people to know they are on top of the current trends. Bottom-line thinking is at work here for Type A people. They often want to see a return on investment for their time and money. Type T's adapt healthier styles of eating, exercise or relaxation because it soothes them. Their return on investment is that they feel better. They're happier when tending to their body, mind and spirit.

Type A leadership junkies thrive on caffeine, fast food, eating on the run or power lunches filled with high-fat, high-carb foods. Often, after work, there are networking events and meetings and dinner may include alcohol and appetizers. Eating habits such as these often do not nourish or nurture your body.

Type T leaders, on the other hand, start to shift their attention to healthier eating habits. Think about it. As you become more aligned with your authentic power and influence, it doesn't make sense to fill your body with fake food, lots of chemical additives and over-processed ingredients. Start with eating fewer processed foods. You don't need to completely overhaul your diet but become aware of the contents of what you're eating. Read the labels more closely. Just make some different choices that are a better fit for you. Eat foods that are real and natural, such as fresh fruits, vegetables and whole grains. Replace soda or energy drinks with water. You will gain better mental clarity and physical stamina. This is nothing you haven't heard or read before; it's just that now is the time to do it.

It helps to remember the phrase "over-processed and underserved." Eating highly processed and fast foods will not serve you in the long run. They may satisfy you temporarily, but they metabolize quickly, turn to fat and leave you wanting more. A study in France by Magalie Lenoir, Fuschia Serre and Lauriane Cantin (Intense Sweetness Surpasses Cocaine Reward, 2007) found that when rats that were addicted to cocaine were given a choice between sweetened water and cocaine, they chose the sweetened water and no amount of an increased dosage of cocaine caused a change—they were more addicted to the power of sugar, even the power of saccharin. So, read labels and also check the labels of any food touting "low fat." The sugar content will be quite high because low fat food simply doesn't taste good, so sugar is used to make it taste better. It's a lose-lose choice—not only are sugar and sugar substitutes addictive, your low fat foods are actually making you fat.

After years of feeling "puffy," struggling to keep the pounds off and dealing with constant congestion, I embarked on the 10-Day Sugar Detox by Dr. Mark Hyman, knowing that I would continue the recommendations beyond the 10-day period. Keep in mind I never met a donut, croissant, baguette or beignet I didn't like. Chips and dip, popcorn or cheese and crackers were often my dinner. I thought an open space in front of the ice cream store was a "sign" that it was okay to get some pralines and cream. After 10 days, I'd lost seven pounds, at eight weeks, 16 pounds and at 12 weeks, a total of 25 pounds. The puffiness was gone and congestion had subsided. And, I have continued on the program with minor modifications. One of my biggest concerns was how to stick to this healthful diet and not be a pain in the #*! You know those annoying people: I don't eat this, and I don't eat that and can you put this on the side and replace xxx with yyy.

A colleague of mine who is the quintessential Type T leader and who transformed his diet and lifestyle had coached me on positive ways to adapt, long before I really made the choice to change. It took me about 15 months to make the commitment to change my eating habits. It took that long to realize that the commitment was to myself and my well-being and not to worry about adapting to other people's standards, reactions or expectations.

I "studied" my friend. If the menu had limited choices, I noticed that he would quietly and politely tell the waiter, "I eat fish, fruits and vegetables. Will you ask the chef what he can prepare for me?" I love this approach because he's clear about what he wants, not what he doesn't want. No fuss, no drama, no explanations.

His example encouraged me to stop saying that "I gave up sugar or I don't eat bread etc." because most people reacted with some horror. Now, if asked, I say I eat what I want. I just don't want most of the foods I used to eat. Really. That doesn't mean I may never eat a loaded baked potato or chocolate cream pie again. I just don't want it now. Some of my friends and colleagues started modifying their eating habits when they saw how healthy I looked and felt. Most have reported that they've lost that craving for sugar. So, I think it's safe to say you will probably have a similar experience.

Nurture Your Body, Mind and Spirit

Exercise is the next component to nurturing and supporting your body. Perhaps a better term than exercise might be "movement." I know—for some, it ranks right up there with giving up dessert, but it's worth it! Take time for a regular physical movement—walking, biking, aerobics, water aerobics, cross-fit, kick boxing, Zumba, Nia, Pilates. Personal and professional transformation can be exhilarating and also stressful. Having an outlet to release stress, tension and anxiety is essential.

I have found that the simple act of walking on a nature trail or even an indoor track can be the best combination for stress relief, meditation and/or problem solving. Exercise or movement leads into feeding your brain and your spirit. Transformational leaders work to find new ways to support their mind and spirit.

You might also look for reading material that supports your vision for the future. Give the traditional business books a break. Consider exploring biographies, contemporary self-help books, New Age or holistic thinkers. The appendix of this book has a list of recommended readings to support you in this process.

Maybe you need to get out of the proverbial box! Find local or online groups or organizations that you want to join that support your personal and or professional transformation. Mastermind groups, church study groups, writers workshops, volunteering for your special interests or causes are all possibilities to support you during this process. For women, there are many organizations and online communities that will provide exposure to contemporary professional and/or spiritual thinking and integration. Feminine Power is one that many women have found useful: www.femininepower.com. For men, The Mankind Project could be a good avenue to consider: www.mankindproject.org.

Other ways to feed your brain and your spirit have to do with the media. What are you watching, and what are you listening to? Do the television shows you're watching or audio choices you make support you in the grieving, healing and positive transformational processes? Television shows like *Shark Tank* or *The Apprentice* may not be the best choices now for building your enlightened, collaborative leadership muscle. Talk radio shows are another form of media that can either support your forward movement or keep you stuck in limited thinking. Your time is valuable, so use media for needed relaxation and for expanding your thinking. Avoiding negative media is one way to do it.

I have to address the artificial energy front before we're done. Watch out for energy drinks loaded with caffeine or sugar and/or other over-the-counter remedies for increased energy, as they are the mainstay of the Type A leader. These will no longer be good choices for you.

If you're on medications now, I'm going to suggest that you consult with a physician who is well versed in integrative medicine and open to natural and holistic approaches, if appropriate. Many women have found that their hormone replacement therapy needs to be adjusted. And some of my clients, men and women, who have been on medication for depression or anxiety have had their prescriptions adjusted during times of transition.

Another option is to consider meditation over medication, if possible. There are CDs for guided meditations, or you can look into church groups, holistic medical and fitness centers that provide group meditations.

If sitting in silence and saying OM isn't your thing, Thomas Moore, author of *Care of the Soul* talks about the importance of engaging in mindless activities. In our fast-paced, tech-driven world, many of the activities of our parents and grandparents are gone or we hire someone to do them for us: making and kneading bread, ironing, washing dishes, chopping wood, weeding gardens, dusting or washing floors. These are what he calls, "mindless activities." And when we perform these mindless activities, Moore says that the mind or soul can wander. It is a time of daydreaming. A time of "nothing." These mindless, repetitive motions allow time for just being. This is the time when creative ideas often spring forth. That's why I like walking on a nature path. It can be mindless, repetitive motion. No potholes or cars to avoid. The sights and smells and sounds calm my heart and boost my creativity.

Have your hobbies fallen by the wayside as a result of climbing the ever-lengthening organizational ladder? Feed your spirit by resuming or starting new forms of self-expression. Gardening, piano or guitar, baking, knitting, pottery, woodworking and painting are ways that some of my clients have centered themselves as they transition to Type T leadership.

And, finally, don't forget playtime! For Type A's, playtime was probably only a memory of childhood and simpler times. Or as an adult, "play" may have become a competitive activity or sport. Consider playing golf or pool, just for the fun of it!

Think about the activities that might bring you joy now. Find time each week or each month for two to four activities that just make you happy. Maybe it's escaping to the movies or taking in live theatre or concerts. Ballet? Symphony? How about attending the local women's roller derby? (You might be amazed at how many people you see there who you know, and, of course, it's always their "first" time!) It could be going to a comedy or improv club or doing something that might be out of the box for you like taking acting lessons. Even that round of golf or a tennis match can be good, as long as the focus is not all about winning but, rather, enjoying the process and enjoyment of just playing.

Again, similar to the emotional journey, as you transition to a healthier lifestyle, there will be people who want to join you on this part of the adventure and those who won't. Don Miguel Ruiz, author of *The Four Agreements,* reminds us in the second agreement "Don't Take Anything Personally." This is your journey, not theirs.

Many clients have reported that they have found their friends and family members to be critical, skeptical, fearful and sarcastic when they have embarked on aligning their body, mind and spirit with a higher purpose.

As excited as you may be about your newfound freedom and the possibilities that lie ahead, the best thing you can do at this time is to limit your conversations about your new ventures with the skeptics in your life. They're just scared or maybe they find you annoying. They love you, and they loved the old you. Or, they may be afraid that you won't love them anymore or that you'll want them to change too.

It's also possible they just want you to stop yammering about your new discoveries. Sometimes there can be a tendency for people going through this kind of transformation to want to change everyone around them. It's like "getting religion" and wanting to convert everyone who crosses your path to new and enlightened ways.

I understand this because my family thought I was nuts, and friends got sick of me yakking away about all the cool things I was learning and doing. If you find that the people in your life start to glaze over or emit heavy sighs, you'll know it's time to back off.

This is a very exciting time, but it's not for the faint of heart. Change takes courage. It's risky and there's always the fear that things may not work out. You have to weigh the alternatives to changing. As one client said, "There's no turning back." And this statement reflects the thoughts of many others. Like them, you may reach a turning point where you can't go back to an environment or lifestyle that feels toxic, negative, stagnant or closed. Or maybe you find it difficult to continue to associate with negative people. That's ok too—it sometimes happens. That's normal too.

It's like swinging on a trapeze—you know that you have to let go of old habits or let go of or limit relationships that negatively affect your health. You have to trust that the bar will be on the other side to grab hold of or that there will be a person on the bar to grab your hands and guide you to the platform. There will be new people and groups that will come into your life that are aligned with your future direction. Trust that there's usually a safety net to catch you if you fall. The support systems may look different from what you had in the past, but trust the process. Trust is imperative, and it can be exhilarating.

The sky is the limit. Explore. Enjoy and celebrate your newfound freedom and path to a healthier new you.

Chapter 4

Type T Means Getting Out of B.E.D.

A couple of years after I had learned and started practicing the power of aligning thoughts, words and actions, I came across a model that focused on accountability and not blaming as a way to get results. Given my past experience in the corporate world, I was responsible for implementing different programs to improve efficiency or communication. After awhile, I was pretty skeptical of models that seemed to be the next big thing and cynically referred to them as "flavor of the month."

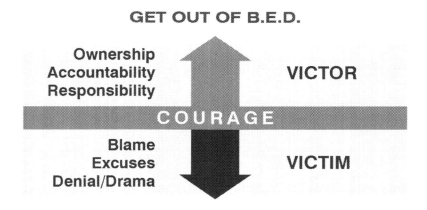

When I read about and saw an illustration of the concepts that evolved into this Get Out of B.E.D. model, my first reaction was: So what? I try not to blame or make excuses. I try to be responsible for my choices. What makes this concept so special or unique? At first, it seemed like there really wasn't anything unique about it.

However, I went back to my first foundational concept about the power of having your thoughts, words and actions clear and aligned. I continued to think about the impact of holding a thought for 17 seconds or more and how whatever is on that vibrational frequency will continue.

I added this concept to my practice of doing The Two Week Challenge whenever I discovered and wanted to try out new ideas. So, in addition to making sure my thoughts, words and actions were clear and aligned with what I wanted, I was listening to my thoughts and words to see if I was truly taking ownership and accountability.

Needless to say, this was a very shocking and humbling experience. I think of myself as a pretty positive person, someone whose word has integrity. But this exercise showed me just how frequently my initial thoughts were based on blaming others and making excuses. I was making excuses or blaming others about 99% of the time! This is not an exaggeration. I'm not talking about just "big stuff." I'm talking about the continuous stream of thoughts running through my head, the constant chatter that never stops. For example, while driving to an appointment, I found myself preparing all the "reasons" why I might be late:

- Delays and detours due to construction.
- Stopping for the inevitable red lights.
- Slow and annoying drivers.

The *real reason* for why I might possibly be late was that I didn't:

- Plan my time.
- I answered a couple more emails or phone calls instead of leaving on time.
- I wasted time on Facebook.

I recommend that you start listening to that chatter in your head right now. Listen to see if you're taking ownership and accountability for what you're thinking, or notice if you are inclined to blame others or make excuses for yourself.

It doesn't make any difference how simple the thought might be. The point is that by habitually blaming others or denying the reality of a situation, we lose power. We allow ourselves to become the victim of someone else's words and/or actions or of a situation.

As you move to transformational leadership, the awareness and practice of taking Ownership, Accountability and Responsibility (O.A.R.) for your Thoughts Words and Actions (T.W.A.) are what will truly set you apart from the traditional ego-driven, Type A leader.

The truth is that you're raising the bar and discovering a higher purpose, a more authentic form of leadership.

To do this, you must practice and work towards mastering the art of O.A.R. for all you think, say and do. This is where true victory and transformation reside. This is the beginning of true leadership on a personal level, as well as professionally.

Warning: I will tell you that 99% of human beings will probably never master the practice of consistently being accountable for their thoughts, words and actions. But it is the intentionality, the persistence and the attempted consistency that will distinguish you from others. Occasionally, a person will say, "I already do that. I take accountability for my thoughts, words and actions and have for a long time."

I think they are delusional and in denial. Just because it's said doesn't mean it's done.

At first it may seem very frustrating to see just how frequently you unknowingly place yourself in the victim role by this repetitive cycle of blaming and making excuses. Remember, though, that if you beat yourself up, you're just perpetuating the negative cycle. Instead, the best thing you can do when you recognize this pattern is to laugh it off and ask yourself, "What can I say or do to take ownership or accountability for this situation?"

I guarantee that you will not only feel better, but you'll see the humor and make a different choice. Here's an example of when I first saw the humor in acknowledging how silly the blame game is.

Several years ago when I worked with a client in El Paso, Texas, I used to stay at a lovely small hotel that served an extensive and wonderful Mexican breakfast buffet. One morning, I spent too much time in my room reading the paper and watching a morning news show. When I finally went to the restaurant, I realized that a Mexican breakfast buffet, no matter how tempting, would not be a good choice when I had a full day of training ahead of me. So I ordered a boiled egg from the menu. Being a special order, it took forever. I became increasingly irritated with the slow service and was almost ready to go into the kitchen and ask what was taking so long. I was going to be late to my appointment because they were so slow! Then it was like a "V-8 moment," when I hit the side of my head and thought, "I'm going to be late because I spent too much time in my room!" Not because it takes 15 - 20 minutes to prepare a special breakfast order.

What it boiled down to (no pun intended) is that we make choices on a moment-by-moment basis. I had made a choice to linger in my room and then to blame the waiter and kitchen staff for my choices. Once you recognize your own patterns of blaming and making excuses, you can start to make different choices that demonstrate ownership and accountability.

I had a client many years ago who was notorious for blaming his staff, or anyone else, for anything and everything. It got to the point that Richard's staff would ignore whatever he had to say. During the coaching process, he saw the impact of this type of communication, not only on himself, but also on his staff and, ultimately, on the success of the organization.

To change this pattern, we agreed that he would tell his staff that he was aware of the impact of his tendency to blame others and that he wanted to change. He told them he was going to practice a new set of skills by taking ownership, accountability and responsibility for his communication, so he could reduce, and hopefully elimi-nate, blaming and making excuses. He warned them that he might stop mid-sentence or mid-thought to concentrate on what he really wanted to say. He asked for their patience and assistance as he practiced his new skills.

At first there was a fair amount of eye rolling and skepticism. But he kept his promise to himself, to me as his coach and to his staff that he wanted to improve their working relationship by improving his communication.

There were times that Richard would stop and say, "That's not what I want to say or what I mean. Let me rephrase that."

Over time, he became more skilled, and his staff was not only supportive, they were genuinely appreciative of the changes and his efforts. They saw how they benefitted from this practice—as awkward as it had seemed at first.

Keep in mind that people can be very generous when they see and hear people openly trying and/or asking for assistance to improve themselves. There's a level of vulnerability, which invokes a degree of compassion that can lead to increased trust.

Again, this is all part of moving to authentic, transformational leadership.

Drama and Courage

There are two other important words on this Get Out of B.E.D. graphic: *Drama* and *Courage*.

"Drama" was added a couple years after using this model with cli-ents and in presentations. I found that whenever there is drama in a situation, you can be sure there is blame and excuses too.

While high drama can be fun, humorous or a good tale to tell, the end result is that it still leaves someone or several people feeling victimized. That may seem like a harsh word for such an "innocent" event. But the bottom line is that the physical and emotional toll can still be the same. Drama can create an environment that isn't safe for people to express concerns or present another point of view. It can also lead to a clique culture that creates exclusion. When people feel excluded from the group or team, interactions can become strained, more toxic or divisive, and the group is deprived of the skills and creativity of the full team. Productivity is lower because of gossip and drama.

An authentic Type T leader consciously strives for inclusion and a safe environment for constructive self-expression. This type of leader will be intentional about having an organizational culture that is free of gossip and rewards inclusion and healthy participation.

"Courage" is an essential characteristic for the transformational leader as well. Taking ownership, accountability and responsibility for thoughts, words and actions takes a huge amount of courage. It does not take any courage to blame others or make excuses when things go wrong.

We live in a society that supports, and often encourages, people to be the victim or to not be accountable. "I ate XXX every day for a year; now I want to sue the company for my bad health," or "Hire XXX lawyer to get you off from that DUI conviction." We are constantly surrounded by people and advertising that encourage us to blame others or not be accountable for our choices. That's another reason why it's important to be aware of the television shows and commercials you're watching, talk radio shows you're listening to or periodicals and newspapers you're reading. When you become aware of the language in the media that is negative, it creates a scarcity mentality, fear-based thinking and/or encourages a victim-like mentality. It's like swimming in a dirty pond or drinking contaminated water. You will learn to avoid it or shut it out.

Don't underestimate the amount of courage it will take when you start practicing ownership, accountability and responsibility. Friends and family can be the most critical because they want you to "be like them." They may view you as being stuck up or acting superior. It's important that you are genuinely being clear, accountable and without judgment. When judgment creeps in, so do blame, excuses and self-righteousness. The reality is that you're on a personal and professional growth path and when you embark on this kind of transformation, it's very hard to turn back.

I mentioned the study at the Institute for Advanced Theoretical Research at the University of Arizona and how emotions can impact our health. One of the things that I found most interesting about the study was that some of the emotions that might be associated with being a Victim or being in B.E.D. (habitual blame, excuses or denial) had a detrimental impact on health. As stated earlier, these negative emotions included shame, anger, guilt, fear and resentment. Conversely, some of the emotions that might be associated with a healthier body and mindset and that could be connected to being accountable and taking responsibility included love, joy, compassion, gratitude and peace.

The study showed that the dividing point between negative and positive emotions and their impact on our bodies was *courage*.

I love that. Courage. Think about the times you've spoken up to defend or represent yourself or another person. It takes courage to speak up for what you believe in. Maybe there were times in the past that you sat back and waited for someone else to take the lead or speak up when witnessing an injustice. Usually there's some regret upon reflection of those times, and we later wish we had taken action or spoken up.

Don't we all want to live in a world where we look out for each other? In a world of healthy boundaries? Healthy communication? All it takes is for one person to start being accountable. All it takes is one person to have the courage to speak up.

The more you are accountable for your choices—thoughts, words and actions, and for taking ownership of the emotions behind them—those around you will change. You cannot wait for agreement or for other people to be the initiators.

The change starts with *you*. Be accountable now, if you want to be the leader you know yourself to be.

Integrity

When I think of this process, of taking ownership and accountability for thoughts, words, actions and emotions, I think about integrity. We must have integrity in our thoughts, words and actions, in order to get the best results. We must have integrity in our personal lives to demonstrate a higher level of leadership and to truly be an authentic leader.

Integrity doesn't mean "right or wrong" or "good or bad." Think of a house or a building. Engineers and architects know that a building needs to have integrity to sustain the weight to go up or extend out.

And so it is with our lives.

You need to have a strong and firm foundation to support your growth. That foundation might be your faith or belief system. And you need the structures in your life to support your expansion. For example, these support structures might be your friends and family, nutrition and exercise programs, spiritual practices, home environment, healthy financial practices. When any one of these is "weak," it can impact or hold back your progress or growth. Earlier, we discussed the importance of healthy relationships during this process. Other examples would be if your home environment is filled with chaos or clutter or if there is a lack of support or resistance from family members to making the change to a healthier home and/or family practices.

No one likes to talk about money, and most people will lie about money, when asked to reveal their income. If you are truly in integrity, that includes having integrity with your finances: paying your bills, paying taxes on time, staying within your budget, managing credit card balances. Being accountable for your income and your expenses. Being accountable for investing or saving for the future. Many people are not being accountable for their financial well being for the future. These people often have a multitude of excuses for not saving money. What are yours?

Have you created any intentions about your financial future, and are you really being accountable by aligning your thoughts, words and actions toward that intention? Or are you making excuses? Are you including other family members for their participation to contributing to a good financial future?

One program that I highly recommend is Dave Ramsey's *Financial Peace University.* For about 10-12 weeks, participants can develop a plan to get out from under credit card debt and create a sustainable savings plan. Perhaps I like it because it's based on being account-able for the choices we make in how we save or spend our dollars.

A personal pet peeve of mine is that many people pride themselves as being independent. My question is, "Are you really independent if your income can not support your lifestyle?" Granted, two income households are more the norm than not. But I have met many people who have started their "own businesses" and are able to only pay the basic business expenses, even several years later, because they have the support of their partner. This is not a sustainable business. This is not being independent. This is a wonderful hobby.

There is a trendy term of being an "authentic" leader. I really don't think a person can be "authentic" if they espouse integrity, for ex-ample, but lack accountability for their finances.

Authenticity is all about alignment. Ownership. Accountability. Integrity.

All of this might seem quite daunting and perhaps impossible. Please realize that it's all a process. It's a process of growth and practice; of learning and failing; of learning and succeeding. There is no one right way and as you transition from a Type A leader to one who is truly transformational, know that it won't happen over-night. It's a process that can take years.

I had a client who was young and professionally immature. She really wanted to be a vice president at a company by the time she was 40, which was five years away. She begged for the formula, the guide or the map to make it happen. Natalie was single-minded, and no one was going to get in her way. She looked the part and commanded everyone around her. Very Type A. As her coach, we talked about the skills and qualities needed to be an effective leader and the responsibilities of being a vice president of an organization. When we discussed the Get Out of B.E.D. model, she assured me that she always took accountability. We discussed how she needed to develop trusted relationships and help her direct reports reach their goals and work collaboratively with her colleagues before she could be considered for a higher-level position. Two weeks later, she informed me that she had done that. What was the next thing for her to do?

For the Type A leader, it's about the checklist. Don't fall into the trap of thinking there is a checklist for becoming a transformational leader.

For the Type T leader, it's about the process. It's the experience, the learning, the journey. It a time for reflection—honoring the past and preparing for the future. During this time of authentic discovery and higher purpose of leadership, there is an interesting combination of intentionality, intuition and spontaneity. And with this can be a newfound level of peace and joy.

The foundational concepts for transforming your life, your leadership and your organization start with understanding power, the stages of power and the transition from one stage to the next. The next step is to align thoughts, words and actions with what you want and to take ownership and accountability for all choices. No blame or excuses! And that includes nurturing your body, mind and spirit as you shift from Type A to the Type T leader you know yourself to be.

From Personal to Professional:
Extending the Transformation

Chapter 5

Creating Intentions and Alignment

Ok, it's time! You are now ready to start transforming to the Type T leadership style in your workplace or other organizations. You are mentally, emotionally and physically primed to make the change. To start, as you now know, one of the cornerstones of successfully transitioning to your more authentic self and to a higher level of leadership is to take ownership and accountability for not only your thoughts, words and actions, but for each step of the process. You've already done this on a personal level when you took The Two Week Challenge, so you know how it works. Applying it in an organization can be a little trickier. Let's take a look at what happens in many organizations when it comes to organizational change, so you can see some of the challenges you may encounter as a Type T leader.

Flavor of the Month

As I mentioned briefly in the previous chapter, when I was in the corporate world, it seemed as though every management team was looking for the next big thing. I called it "Flavor of the Month."

Remember the *One Minute Manager, Seven Habits of Highly Effective People, TQM* and *Process Re-engineering?* Now we have *Six Sigma, Lean Management*— you name it— anything to make managers better listeners, better leaders, more efficient, better communicators. It always seemed that just as a process was being implemented, senior leaders would deem that it wasn't working and start the process of looking for the next big thing. In the words of Jim Collins of *Good To Great*, the "flywheel" of new behaviors had hardly taken hold, and the wheel would come to a screeching halt and then have to reverse to adapt to something new.

What I found was that most managers and employees who had been around for a while would lie low and murmur under their breaths, "This too shall pass."

Usually, when managers would change jobs or retire, they would cart out boxes of three-ringed binders that they had accumulated over the years, sometimes decades, thinking that maybe someday they would use these binders as a reference for pearls of wisdom. Probably not.

What did happen during this process of implementing the next big thing, the next flavor of the month, was that the leadership team was adding to the pattern of distrust and disengagement among the employees. Senior management could pat themselves on their backs and tell their board about the big initiative, without ever having a real "champion" for the process or knowledge of what it was supposed to do or fix. And of course, whatever it was designed to change certainly did not apply to them. In many situations, the designated senior management champion rarely attended the meetings that were designed to establish outcomes or an implementation plan that would create buy-in from the troops. Sadly, many of these so-called champions would send their administrative assistant to take notes for them and fill them in on the progress. This is not said to be disrespectful of either senior management or assistants, but this approach to the process lacked integrity and accountability.

Meanwhile, many employees would mock the next big thing, knowing they would continue to do what they've always done and pretend like the new program was really great. Some people would become passive-aggressive about it and do what they could to subvert or block any change or progress, without being detected, of course.

As a human resource executive, I was in a double bind: carrying out the executive direction (aka—whim) and spending lots of time and money with consultants, while knowing the execs were abdicating results to someone, or anyone, else—which was usually ME. I also knew that I had to be a good corporate soldier and sell the project to the rest of the management team and employees and then deal with their understandable resistance.

Many of you have seen that there can be a real dichotomy in organizations when it comes to "bottom line thinking" and decision making. Keep in mind that the Flavor of the Month mentality isn't confined to human resource initiatives. Consider the new and improved marketing and advertising programs, enhanced products and/or service lines and especially the new technologies that are the next big thing. Many of the initiatives that I just described are implemented to be "politically correct" or for the appearance of being enlightened or progressive. But there's no real "buy-in" from the leadership team to make sure it works. So this is an example of a bottom line driven company being inconsistent with making choices that impact the bottom line. I've always maintained that any initiative that management isn't prepared to reinforce is a huge waste of time and money. Many costly marketing and technology initiatives are started, only to be derailed or replaced by another, bigger, "shinier" program. The cost of the software or hardware and time spent by IT professionals can be staggering. Or, it could be a branding or marketing initiative. And when the leaders don't see a rapid return on investment, they say, "We're going in another direction" and hundreds of thousands of dollars or millions are lost. But for some reason, bottom-line thinkers find a way to justify their decisions. Unfortunately, what is left in the wake of these initiatives are the employees who dedicated their time and talent to make a project successful, only to be told: "Never mind. We're going in another direction." The Type A bottom-line thinker would say, "So what? They're getting paid to do a job; what difference does it make if the project is stopped?" But the stop and start of employee energy, engagement and creativity takes a toll. Trust and commitment is diminished.

Creating Intentions

It became increasingly difficult for me to balance and be account-able in this executive role and position, as well as be accountable and have integrity with myself. It became a personal and professional standoff. I found it very uncomfortable.

And, it just happened to hit at the point when I was in the early days of my transition from Type A to Type T. In the mid-1990's, I embarked on an extensive, and intensive, personal and professional growth program, and my journey to authentic leadership escalated. I was learning about integrating accountability and integrity in all areas of my life. Early on in my studies, I was asked to create my future for the next 150 years, to describe my legacy. What did I want it to be? It was the first time that I began to think about being accountable for who I am, not just in the moment, but also for perpetuity. It was somewhat of a daunting thought. How was I contributing to my communities? Was I consistent, congruent and accountable across all areas of my life?

That was my first real exposure to creating intentions. I was being asked to create my *future* intentions. Who was I and what did I want to contribute to my current and future communities? So I ask you now: What are *your* intentions? Who are your communities?

Who do you want to be as a leader? As a parent, a sibling, a neighbor or leader in your community?

As I describe the process that I went through, always keep this question in mind: What are your intentions?

As I embarked on creating my legacy, my first reaction was "I have no idea." This was the first time I was truly integrating my personal and professional life, which is fundamental to becoming a Type T leader. As I allowed my mind to explore possibilities, I eventually realized that I wanted to create a process that would make a difference for people and for organizations, where they wouldn't have to remember seven habits or six steps or five keys. It would be a process that would make a difference for people that would *empower* them with knowledge, skills, information or resources that could be *regenerating*, as in "pay it forward" and *sustainable*—long lasting, not a fad and definitely not flavor of the month.

I had seen way too many models that failed. Either the model was flawed or the people who were charged with implementing the model in an organization weren't committed or accountable to make it work. Either way, a high price was paid, financially and emotionally. When organizations take on major initiatives to change a culture or improve leadership skills, only to stop them a year or two later, it takes a huge toll on the health of an organization—individual by individual and cumulatively as an organizational culture. It can become a culture of cynics or apathy. Certainly not a healthy culture of quality performance and productivity, contribution and profitability. Does this sound familiar?

I share this because when you start creating your intentions on a personal level, most times you have no idea how to implement them. I had no idea what "my model" would look like if I were going to empower people and have it be regenerating and sustainable. All I knew was that I *wanted* to create a model or process that would be easy to remember and could make a difference for people and organizations.

And because I didn't know how to do it, I asked myself "Am I crazy?" many times.

Yet in the early stages of creating my intention, each time I thought I was nuts to embark on this possibility, I was introduced to people, resources and information that were very unlike the people I had known in my corporate circles. They, in turn, were introducing me to more people and more information and resources, none of which had anything to do with traditional business models or the conventional wisdom that I had been exposed to throughout my career. After a while, I trusted and realized the information and resources had *everything* to do with my intention of creating a process that would make a difference for people and organizations.

To say that it was an exciting time is an understatement.

I was learning things about quantum physics and neuroscience (albeit what I would call a *"Reader's Digest* version.") It was thrilling to learn about the power of the brain and about the vibrational energy we discussed in Chapter 2. Imagine! Hold a thought for 17 seconds or more and whatever is on that frequency will come back to you? Wow! I had no idea how powerful our thoughts are!

During this time, I was learning that we produce and manifest results based on what we think, what we say and what we do—and in that order. I learned that it's the power of the emotion behind our thoughts, words and actions (T.W.A.) that allows us to achieve results. This is far different than how a typical Type A leader gets results. A Type A leader often pushes through; it's all about action to get results, doing, doing, doing! The Type T leader steps back and first aligns thoughts with intentions, aligns words with thoughts and intentions and *then* aligns actions to get the desired results.

There was a book and a movie that came out in 2006 called *The Secret*, by Rhonda Byrne, which refers to the Law of Attraction. While I was not a big fan of the book, it did create more of a mainstream awareness of this phenomenon. And if you never heard of it before, don't worry. You probably weren't watching *Oprah* because it seemed there was always someone on the show connected with the book. Frankly, I thought it was a little fluffy and preferred the scientific research that explained the same concepts in a more logical, pragmatic way. Plus, when I was introducing the concepts in the early 2000's, many of the people I was talking to about this concept were in corporate workshops. While many were resistant or reluctant at first, they more readily accepted or would consider the concepts if they were based in science, not fluff.

So the power of T.W.A. became a foundational concept for what was emerging as a new model for making a difference for people. It was the first step toward my intention of creating a process that would make a difference for people *and* organizations. And, of course, I had to practice and test it, relentlessly.

Since results are based on thoughts, then words and then actions, I began to examine what happens if one of the three components is missing. For example, I might decide I want to lose five pounds. But then I would jump on the couch with some Ben and Jerry's or go through the drive- through and say, "Can you supersize that for me?" I'd never lose those five pounds because what I was doing was inconsistent with what I was thinking and saying.

Remember when I talked about The Two Week Challenge? This is the perfect time to really examine what you're thinking. Are your thoughts, words and actions really aligned with your intentions? Are your intentions clear? Are your intentions consistent? If anything is missing or out of whack, you won't get the results you want.

Applying these concepts sounds simple and they really aren't hard, but it takes intentionality and consistency. It's important to have clear intentions about what you want, not what you don't want. So many times our focus is on what we don't want: "I don't ever want to work for a boss like that again!" or "I don't want to hire people who can't get along." The net result is that we still get what we're focused on—even if it's something we don't want. It's like the example of the Red Light and Green Light Days in the second chapter. What you're focused on is what you get—whether it's what you want or not.

As I work with people who are getting clear about what they want, oftentimes they struggle with identifying what that "looks like." So

I recommend the George Costanza approach. Remember George from *Seinfeld*? George was the consummate loser—nothing ever went his way, except in one episode when he decided to do the opposite of everything he would normally do. After all, it couldn't be any worse than it was. And that was the day that he met a great girl, got a great job and everything went *great*.

So if you're stuck and unclear about what you want or have trouble identifying the intentions of what you want, take the George Costanza approach. In a column on the left side of a piece of paper, write down all the things you don't want. Then, in the right hand column, write down whatever the opposite of that would be. Keep writing until you feel like you've hit the core of what you want.

Here are a few examples of transforming negative intentions into positive ones:

I don't want to be in a dead-end job.	*I intend to have a job that uses my skills and abilities and can make a difference.*
	I intend to have a job that has a good career progression with increasing salary potential.
	I intend to have a job that has transferrable skills to other jobs and industries.

These concepts can also be readily applied in an organizational setting. Just as individuals create their reality through their thoughts, words and actions, so do organizations. The results are manifested in what is referred to as corporate culture.

How many times have you seen or experienced organizations that tout that their "employees are their greatest asset," yet their actions are glaringly the opposite? I had the opportunity to work for an organization that espoused this platitude; it was engraved on plaques around the building and employees wore little laminated badges that reminded them they were a valued asset. Despite the outward show of this core value, the door to the human resources office was locked during the day and had a sign that said "Closed. Open 10 - 2." Apparently, the employees were only valued during that window of time. Another company that adopted this trendy cliché regularly changed the sales staff compensation programs mid-year, making it virtually impossible for them to reach their sales goals. There are a myriad of examples like these, where organizations start out with a good idea, such as valuing their employees, but are not accountable for implementing policies and practices that are consistent with the message.

As you can see, it is equally, if not more, important that organizational leaders strive to align core values with operational communication and practices. They must be diligent, persistent and consistent in this practice in order to maximize employee engagement, productivity, profitability and customer satisfaction.

Perhaps, as you're moving from Type A to Type T, you're noticing a lack of alignment with your values and the organizations for which you work. This is one of those situations that can lead you to, again, think you're crazy and perhaps a bit of a misfit. The best thing you can do upon this realization is to focus and align your thoughts, words and actions around that which you can control. For example, if you are a manager of a department or projects that require cross-functional coordination and collaboration, focus your energies on creating the communication and environment that you want and that you think will achieve the best results for the good of the employees, the organization and the people you're serving.

Hopefully, at this point you are beginning to see how your personal transformation impacts your organization and how the steps for alignment will be quite similar.

Chapter 6

Closing the Past and Creating the New You

Before you can truly define your new vision and purpose, it's a good idea to get very clear about what's *not* working in your life. Work is a significant part of your life and if you aren't doing what feels "right" to you, there will be a disconnect. It's time to look inside yourself to identify who you want to be in order to find your organizational "fit." This process helps you expand to your transformed lifestyle to Type T leadership.

This is the "George Castanza" approach with a different perspective. It can be hard to accept that there are responsibilities, career requirements, aspects of our lifestyles and even people that just aren't working in our lives—not the right fit. To help with this, I not only challenge and encourage you to do the exercise that follows, but to be completely honest and as thorough as possible. This exercise is for you alone to help identify what you want to transition towards—your dreams, your goals, your life changes.

On the left side of the page, write down all of the things you don't want, don't like, aren't willing to settle for, don't want to repeat or do again, behaviors you want to stop or change, the kind of work you don't want to do and the kind of people you don't want to work with or be around. It may be a long list, but all those elements matter.

What are the feelings associated with those things you don't want in your life? On the right side, write down all the words that come to mind about how you *feel* doing that work, being with those people, etc. List as many emotions as you can that reflect how you feel.

While this may be painful to think about, it will help you become very clear about all the things you do want in your life. In addition, you will have identified the emotions that you want to avoid and how you want to feel when you have the things that you want.

This will undoubtedly require going back into your past, as those decisions and actions created your current situation. When you are in the process of transforming, you don't want to repeat the negatives from the past or the present or rub up against those "sharp objects" that we talked about when we shed ourselves of old habits. Use them to discern the changes you want to make. Don't hesitate to look back as you create your list, as it will help you find the causes of your dissatisfaction.

The next step is to create another T-Chart on a separate piece of paper. This time, refer back to your first list and on the left side, write what you *do* want or the opposite of what you had written on the first page. Sometimes it can take several attempts to nail down exactly what it is you do want, so just keep writing till you find the one, or ones, that hit home for you. And, like the previous exercise, write down how you will feel when that happens. There may be multiple words such as "joy, freedom, peace of mind, self confidence . . ." As you do this, you will feel yourself becoming lighter, more optimistic, hopeful and confident that change is possible. Remember, it's the power of the emotion behind the thought that attracts more of what's on that vibrational frequency. You want that "giant magnet" to be attracting good, joyous feelings!

Finding Closure on the Past

Now you've identified the causes of your unhappiness, the emotions attached and identified the things that you do want and how you'll feel when that happens. The next step is to close that period of your life out, so you can move on. To help illustrate this, here's an example.

I remember a client, Ben, telling me he thought he was crazy that he wanted to leave the business he helped cofound. In this situation, he was the person who provided 100% of the financial backing for a close friend. They became business partners in a new venture that was her passion, not his. It was a longstanding friendship, and he was ready for a change, so he left a high-paying corporate sales job to assist his friend and take a stab at being an entrepreneur. Five years later, his business partner still had no financial skin in the game, and her credit rating was such that she could not get her own credit. Ben, on the other hand, had maxed out his credit cards, dipped into his long-term savings, and his life partner had changed jobs to earn more, since Ben's income was substantially lower due to his entrepreneurial endeavors.

After telling me the details of this venture, and with tears in his eyes, he asked, "Am I crazy to be upset about this?" Apparently, his friend had convinced him he was unreasonable when he asked her to find funding to buy him out.

I assured him that he wasn't crazy and, in fact, he was really funding another person's dream, not his—no wonder he wasn't happy. When asked to describe how he felt, Ben could barely speak. He said he would break down completely if he really acknowledged the totality of his feelings. So, to help him realize he wasn't crazy or unreasonable, I outlined a few of the emotions I thought he might be feeling, so he could come to grips with the situation.

First was sadness about the loss of friendship with his once-close friend. They were barely on speaking terms after years of a vibrant and healthy friendship. Other emotions associated with that loss were betrayal, grief, disappointment.

He was disappointed in himself. He was disappointed that he had not been stronger in standing up for himself and for putting a financial strain on his relationship with his life partner of 20 years. Their savings were gone and would take years to rebuild.

It was very sad. All in the name of friendship. A friendship that was not reciprocated or appreciated.

So, we started working on appreciating and acknowledging all that he had done in the interest of friendship and the experiment of being an entrepreneur. It takes courage to do that, and he gave it his best effort.

You see, underneath it all, Ben felt like a failure. It was important for him to see that in so many ways he was not a failure, but, rather, a person who was bold, loving and supportive. And that while the situation may have gone on too long or spun way out of control, his intentions were good and honorable. There was a lot to admire in this man. And there is a happy ending to this story! Ben, his business partner and their accountant developed a payment plan so he could recoup his investment. While he's still a silent partner in the business, he has embarked on a new entrepreneurial venture that makes his heart sing! The new business is aligned with things that make him happy (travel) and express his natural skills and abilities (planning, sales and marketing).

It's hard to build a new future or new vision when there is no closure to the past. Closure is not about saying, "What's done is done," and moving on. That's for people hanging on to a Type A approach to problem solving, decision making and closure. Soldier on! Slog through it! Power on and don't look back.

Here's the difference between the Type A and Type T leader. The latter will take time for reflection. Time to acknowledge what went well and what could have been done differently.

Closure at this stage is not a transactional process. It's transformational—transforming the negative into ways to learn and appreciate the value of the experience. Closure must include addressing the emotional issues you identified by acknowledging them for what they are—no more, no less. No drama, no victimization. Having and acknowledging these emotions is not a sign of weakness or of being a victim, but rather a bold and courageous step in the right direction. By taking ownership of the sadness, the grief, the disappointment, you can close that chapter, to move on and start to create something new. Ben, being a Type T leader, was able to work through the sadness and have closure to the past and create something new that is aligned with his future self.

Albert Einstein said the definition of insanity is doing the same thing over and over and expecting different results. This strategy of putting real closure to emotional upset in this way can be a preventive approach to not being in this type of situation again.

It doesn't mean that you won't experience sadness or disappointment again. It just means that you will recognize it faster and be able to make another choice. Ultimately, it always comes back to making choices, including the emotions that we choose to experience.

So take a look back over the past 12 - 18 months and look at all you've experienced in various areas of your life. The good, the bad and the ugly. Take some time to acknowledge the emotions associated with those experiences and reflect on what you've learned.

By taking the time to do this, you will put some closure on that part of your life so that you can start creating a new path.

We've spent a lot of time exploring what's working and not working in your life and by now you're probably thinking, "OK! Let's get on with it! What do I do now, and how do I move forward outside of my personal life?"

That may still be a little of Type A hanging on and coming through, but that's ok. Old habits die hard . . .

And, any leftover Type A won't stand a chance, as this is the most fun and creative part of the process. It's the time that we will be recreating, redefining, transforming and aligning your vision and purpose for your life right now and the foreseeable future.

Defining Who You Want to Be

Up until now, you've probably moved along in life based on the opportunities or setbacks encountered and did the best you could at each step, hoping to make decisions that were optimum at the moment. You probably made decisions regarding your education, jobs, relationships, marital status and children. Many times people make decisions based on their parents' or spouse's or bosses' expectations or who they think they should be for their kids or who they think their kids want them to be. Do you fit any of these categories? Or, maybe you have been living and acting on the dreams and expectations that were set when you were in your 20's or 30's. Perhaps you feel like you've been living on autopilot for the past 25 or 30 years. And now you're saying, "Whose life is it, anyway?"

Now is your time to choose. I use the word "choose" very deliberately, rather than the word "decide." Here's why: Think of all the words that end with "cide." Suicide, genocide, pesticide, homicide, insecticide, herbicide just to name a few.

See a trend here? All these words are about ending, killing off, dying etc. In fact, "cide" actually comes from the Latin meaning of killer or to kill—and we're not creating positive vibrations with those thoughts! It's better to choose. Be intentional. Be deliberate.

We want to use words that are reflective of what we want, not what we don't want. Just as we explored earlier, we want to be deliberate in our choice of words as we create our future. By making choices, we are able to continue that process of making different ones, adding to them or modifying them, so they work with, not against, our new direction. We don't have to throw the baby out with the bath water and feel like we have to start all over because of a bad, dead-end decision or something that didn't turn out the way we'd hoped.

Now, know that your choices can and will be intentional, not reactionary. Your choices can and will be proactive, aligned with who you are now, not who others expect you to be or want you to be. So often, as we lived our Type A lives, we had to maintain an image of who we thought we should be to be successful and recognized in the eyes of other people. Our measures and benchmarks were external. There was often incongruity between our work life, personal life, family life and spiritual life. Perhaps you used to say: "I'm different when I'm at home or with my family than at work. My personal life stops when I walk through the doors at work. I can't let things going on at home affect work and can't talk about it here." Can you see how these statements created a separation of self? Instead of being an integrated, whole person, you were a compilation of several parts, all compartmentalized and each focused on an external definition of success. My role as a wife or husband. My role as a corporate leader. How I want to be seen as a community leader. Who I think I should be as a parent.

Now, when transitioning to a higher level of more authentic leadership and purpose, it is an internal, personal process. Transformational leadership is about personal alignment and integration. When you are clear about who you want to be as a holistic and integrated person, there is no separation or distinction between your work, home, community and/or your spiritual choices. The areas of your life can flow more easily and effortlessly. There is less internal and external struggle and more acceptance because there is more integrity and alignment in your choices. I say less struggle and more acceptance internally because you are at peace with the alignment and integration of who you know yourself to be. There is less struggle and more acceptance externally because your family, friends and colleagues, who went with you on your journey, and even those who weren't sure at first, can now sense your peace of mind and respond to that. Even better, other people won't have to guess which role you're playing and can trust your choices more thoroughly without fear of repercussion.

Key Words for Authenticity

The best way to start the introspection needed for authenticity and transformation is by creating a laundry list of words that define who you want to be as a Type T leader—at work, home and in your community. What do you want to be known for? What qualities and characteristics represent your true self and that you want to demonstrate on a regular basis? How do you want to feel? Go back and review your "opposites" list from the previous exercise.

Just write as many words as you can, without judging or filtering. Ideally, you will list 20 or more words. If you hit a stumbling block, think about the people you have known whom you admire or for whom you have profound respect. What qualities did they consistently demonstrate? What could you reliably count on them for, and would you like to emulate or demonstrate the related traits? Here are some words to consider to help you get started:

Professional	Passionate	Having integrity
Sensitive	High quality	Empathetic
Joyous	Respectful	Team player
Caring	Fun	Of service
Empowering	Compassionate	Happy
Bold	Inspiring	Motivating
Creative	Thought provoking	Flexible
Courageous	Patient	Visionary
Curious	Inquisitive	Open
Trusting	Reliable	Accepting

The next step is to identify and focus on the top five or seven words that resonate the most for you. Going through this process of elimination is essential. It helps you really discern and choose who you want to be, intentionally and deliberately.

Keep in mind that it doesn't mean that you have to demonstrate these qualities now or even know how to demonstrate these qualities yet.

I have had many clients over the years, who have gone through this process without a clue as to how to be the person they intended to be. But their desire and intentionality made it possible.

Remember Jean—the steamroller who didn't like her colleagues? When we went through this process, we created a list of words that was unique to her and who she wanted to be as a leader, not only at work, but also as a parent and friend.

Here are some of her words:

Trusting   Empowering   Team player   Caring   Joyous

Then we embarked on the process of defining each of her key words. For example:

What would it look like if she were being trusting or joyous?

What would it sound like if she were being empowering or a team player?

What would people be seeing when she demonstrated these qualities?

What would she be hearing when she demonstrated these qualities?

How would she be feeling when she demonstrated these qualities?

How did she want others to feel when they were around her?

What results would be present or produced when she incorporated these qualities in her life?

Jean could see the vision, and she could hear what it sounded like. She immersed herself in the totality of the feeling and being the kind of leader who she knew her authentic self to be.

At this point it's important to back up a little and revisit the deliberate creation of the Type A leader from the intentionality of one who is Type T. When people are moving to Type A leadership, it's very externally focused. Common recommendations and training would say, "Fake it till you make it." "Act as if . . . " was once a popular phrase, meaning you should act as if you've already attained the level of success that you are seeking. Many of you may remember those days. It may have seemed like you were always looking over your shoulder to make sure no one noticed that you were a "fake" or would be "found out." I have heard from more than one executive that they feared "being found out" or that they weren't really as good as they pretended to be. Basically, it was their lack of confidence in their new role that was doing the talking. Most of these same people were qualified "on paper" but lacked the confidence with the new status, the recognition and being considered the expert, even though that's exactly what they were driving towards. For the Type A leader, it's all about ME! Look at ME! See what I have done!

The Type T's journey into the deliberate creation of their new vision and purpose is exactly the opposite: it's about a higher purpose, being authentic, being a contributor, being of service and making a difference for others. "About me" now becomes: How can *I help* you? How can *I contribute* to a better outcome for the good of all?

So, back to Jean. She practiced being the leader she knew herself to be. She was diligent and persistent and consistent in her focus. She was unlearning old behaviors and practicing new ones. It's like going to the gym and using new equipment or learning a new sport or new musical instrument. At first, it's awkward and uncomfortable, but then it becomes "natural/normal."

One of the ways I coached her to adapt her new way of thinking was to practice asking herself questions like:

What would I say if I were being trusting?

What would I do if I were being a team player?

What would I be thinking if I were being empowering and less controlling?

I guarantee you that if you make it a practice to start asking yourself these questions, based on your own key words, the outcomes will be totally different than if you responded in your usual manner.

And that's how it was for Jean. Before responding with her usual snarky answer, she'd mentally ask herself several questions, testing her key words to see which response was best for the situation. She would make sure her vibrational energy was aligned with her intention. Then, calmly, she would address the situation at hand, deliberately and intentionally turning into a Type T leader.

People immediately began to see a difference in how she responded. Her colleagues, her boss and her team started experiencing her new approach and, of course, at first were skeptical. Over time, they began to trust her sincerity and new relationships developed that were constructive and team focused. Her family also noticed a difference, and even her ex-husband became more conciliatory with her new approach.

After about a year and a half of practicing her key words, it became second nature to her. I later worked with several of her colleagues, who all remarked how different she was and how terrific she was to work with. About two years after we worked together, she was promoted again. But, this time it was based on her ability to collaborate and build teams, getting results through teamwork, not coercion. Success was sweet for everyone involved.

I lost track of Jean for several years and about eight years after we worked together, I received a Linked-In invitation to connect from her. She had moved out of state and been promoted to a higher position at a much larger institution.

No doubt she brought her new skills set and talents to her new job. A lot of people think that people can't change. They can if they have the desire and purpose for the change. Having a structured process to reclaim your authentic self and commitment to the process will ensure success.

Another client, who was particularly high strung, found this exercise to be somewhat challenging, to start. Pat was a young mother at the time, highly emotional, perhaps due to lack of sleep and the stress of being the primary wage earner for the family. She was in a high-pressure sales management job, and her team had to produce results each month. Her edginess and emotional outbursts were really hindering her not only in her job, but negatively affecting her team's success and results.

When we worked together to identify her key words, the top four that she identified for who she wanted to be as a leader, a wife and mother were:

Compassionate   Respectful   Professional   Serene

Keep in mind that she demonstrated none of these qualities at home, at work or with family or friends when we first started working together.

We went through the same process as described with Jean. Pat created and immersed herself in her visualizations and auditory scenarios for both at work and at home. She described feeling a great sense of peace of mind when she reviewed her visualizations and could see herself responding with these positive emotions. For a more constant connection to her words, she created a screensaver for her computer where they creatively scrolled across, as a daily reminder of who she wanted to be as a leader. She placed the words in large letters on a sign that was on the back of her door. If someone came to talk to her confidentially and with the door closed, she could be reminded of the words by simply and occasionally looking beyond the person to the door to be reminded of being compassionate or calm or respectful or professional. Pat took this seriously, and it paid off for her and others.

People began to feel they were receiving special attention from her. She was listening to them in ways she had never listened before. The team responded favorably, and sales goals were met and exceeded on a regular basis.

Her kids were calmer and happier—and so was she. Her husband felt more respected, and their relationship improved dramatically.

Success! Aahhh.

It's interesting how, over the years, I have occasionally met and worked with people who have fallen into success. They had no particular plan or vision for their career. They had no particular passion that they felt needed to be expressed or fulfilled. And, yet, they have risen to the tops of their organizations and seem relatively happy.

Jack is a good example of a very successful executive of a highly specialized financial services organization. What makes his story interesting is how his career started. Fresh out of college, at the age of 23, Jack became the marketing director for Ringling Brothers/ Barnum Bailey Circus. He fell into the job by a stroke of luck and literally ran away and joined the circus.

No kidding. How many of us have said we'd like to quit our jobs, run away and join the circus? Sounds like a dream job, doesn't it? Travel the world. Meet and work with interesting people. How many of us get to work with people who are *paid* to be clowns or are shot out of a cannon or swallow swords?

But alas, like many jobs, working for the circus had long hours, lots of travel, preventing any kind of normal social life or real dating prospects for this young man. There were short deadlines and im- mense pressure to fill the seats night after night with an art form and entertainment platform that was being eclipsed by more trendy and contemporary forms of entertainment.

And so it seemed, for Jack, that the next most exciting industry to explore was, ironically, financial services. Fast forward thirty years, and he's a hugely successful executive who has earned a solid reputation in a unique field and engineered several mergers and acquisitions, positioning his organization as a leader in its industry. Did he plan this? No. Did he aspire to this? No. Did he have a passion for financial services? No.

But what he did do was take deliberate steps in a forward direction with each and every opportunity presented. Keenly aware of his strengths and the things that bring him joy in his work, he knew that this was the perfect position for him. And, he just happened to land there, and it was a great fit for the long haul.

One of my clients, Phil, experiencing a completely different situation than Jack, had become his father's successor in the family business. When we first met, he was "flatlined" in his career, his work and his marriage. It wasn't good. It wasn't bad. It was a matter of keeping the wheels turning, at work and at home. For Phil, "There was no joy in Mudville." He felt a huge obligation to his parents to continue the family business, which was successful but required a sizeable investment of time, money and resources for modernization. And his young family counted on him as well. Everything at home seemed like a struggle and a hassle. He was weary at home and at work, and he was only 45 years old.

For Phil, it was about creating purpose and vision within an existing business structure. It was about rediscovering joy and breathing in life, first for himself, then for his family and business.

Shortly after being certified as a life coach, I learned the importance of asking clients about their physical and mental health, as well as their current medications. And, I frequently ask about their spiritual practices.

In earlier chapters, we've explored the aspects of having mental, physical, and emotional stamina and the structures to support transformation and tending to the body, mind and spirit. Phil was a prime candidate for this discussion. He was overweight, chewed tobacco and had limited physical stamina due to chronic exhaustion and stress.

It's hard to create new possibilities and new vision *and* authentic leadership with all of this going on.

His first assignment was a medical check-up, specifically to address his exhaustion and "flatline" view of the world. In addition to being diagnosed with mild depression, Phil was diagnosed with severe sleep apnea. A C-PAP machine and mild anti-depressant made a world of difference and enabled him to start a walking program. This transitioned to walking with his wife each night and, eventually, they were joined by the kids on their bikes. The increase in vitality immediately made for a better home life. Living in a somewhat rural community, Phil and his family previously were known because of the family business, but not seen very much. The nightly walks created a new social aspect to their lives that had been missing.

At work, he had a better attitude and more energy to do some creative problem solving. We were able to create a new vision for the business and action plans to achieve his goals and vision. He was able to focus on hiring the right people to streamline efficiencies and improve profitability. As Phil's energy and enthusiasm increased, his team became more engaged in their jobs, which resulted in better service in the field.

And, as the operations became more effective, Phil was able to direct his energy into his personal goals and vision and the things he really loved—making business deals and flying airplanes. His community involvement also increased, and he became an active member in civic organizations and philanthropic endeavors.

Over the next couple of years, the company doubled in revenue, and Phil had introduced contemporary technologies in a stodgy, traditional industry in a rural community. His contributions to the community were quiet, but powerful, and he became a civic leader, as well as the president of a statewide industry association.

Moving to authentic leadership at work, at home, in his community and in his industry, had required improving his health. When we completed our work together, Phil also had lost over 50 pounds, was bicycling regularly and had stopped chewing tobacco.

I love happy endings like that.

Chapter 7

The New Normal

You can now see that as you discover your higher purpose of leadership so you can truly make an impact on an organization or your communities, you need to establish your authentic self first. The purpose of this process is to not emulate anyone else or copy other leaders' styles. Instead, it's to develop true peace with who you are first, so you can bring forth your own best skills and talents to make a difference in the world. You're at a point in your life where you've experimented trying to be someone you're not or be like your mentor or favorite boss and now know that it just doesn't work.

At the same time that you have been going through your stages of self-discovery and changing on the inside, the external world has changed dramatically. Contemporary leaders are now expected and required to adapt to shifting external factors and help their organizations adapt as well.

In order to look at the external factors that have changed our world, we need to briefly go back to 2008 because it was a benchmark year for many reasons. And upon reflection, most people would agree that the rate, pace and magnitude of external changes that have taken place since then are unprecedented. For the majority of us, these changes were beyond our control, yet our lives have never been the same since. In January of 2010, I introduced a new keynote called "The New Normal." At that time, I referenced the major changes that had taken place between 2000 and 2010. Little did I know the rapid progression of changes yet to come.

By 2014, just four years after introducing The New Normal, I had revamped this program 10 -15 times and only highlighted changes between 2008 and 2014. The name of the program changed as well to Living The New Normal because we had to adapt to the collapse of the financial and housing markets, the dissolution of major institutions and changes in technology and legislation. Our lives would never be the same. Here are a few of the significant events since 2008:

- Bernie Madoff; bailouts and industries collapsing; BP oil spill.
- Scandals: politics, religion, sports.
- Social media and technology (FaceBook, Twitter, texting, Pinterest, Instagram).
- Health care and financial reforms.
- Greed, waste and excess.
- Sandy Hook, Boston bombing, Hurricane Sandy.
- Emergence of Tea Party, government sequester, gridlock and shutdown.

Very few people have not been affected by at least one or more of these events. The economic recovery has been slow and even if you didn't personally experience a significant loss during this time, you probably know people who did. And for many, these changes meant changes in priorities and how time and money were spent. Maybe a vacation was delayed or turned into a "staycation." Or, instead of buying a new home, money was invested in a home remodeling project. Maybe new skills had to be gained to adapt to the current job market. The point is that all of our lives and our families' lives and the lives of the people in our communities have been affected by a loss of some sort.

In previous chapters, we've explored how your life has changed, so take a minute to think about changes since 2008. Use the time to reflect on how things have changed for you, your family and your work colleagues. It may be worthwhile to also write down the impact as a reminder of how life can change with little warning.

Now, let's take a look at your workplace or the organizations where you volunteer. Very few organizations have not been affected by the massive changes that have occurred since 2008. How have things changed in your organization during the same time period? What new technologies have been introduced? How have products and services shifted? Are there new demands on the employees or volunteers that have required changes in operating procedures?

There are significant external factors that have impacted organizations since 2008. For example, most industries have new regulations that require increased compliance. There are new technologies and ways to communicate with customers, employees and vendors. We live in a more global society, where work can be performed in a virtual environment, halfway around the world. Jobs are no longer "8 to 5" because people are having conference calls at midnight to coordinate with virtual teams or employees who reside on other continents.

I've worked with some rural medical facilities around the United States and while these communities may appear to still be living in the land of Andy Griffith, Aunt Bee and Mayberry, they are being forced to adapt to new technologies to stay in business. Health care reform and electronic medical records may be forced upon them, but new forms of health care delivery systems such as telemedicine may be the only way to stay in existence because attracting and retaining a qualified medical staff in remote and rural areas is extremely difficult.

Mergers and acquisitions have allowed some companies to stay in business, but they are requiring organizations to become like "blended families." When companies merge, they have to adapt and blend, creating new cultures and, oftentimes, new processes, new forms of communication and streamlined products or services.

Perhaps one of the biggest impacts on the workplace is the influx of Generation Y, also referred to as the Millennial Generation. The people in this age group were born between 1980 and 2000. They have never known a world without computers. The demographics of this group are unlike any previous generation, and for the Boomers (born approximately between 1946 and 1965), we better get used to the idea that our boss may be the same age as our kids. And we better get over it fast, if we're going to succeed in a corporate setting or even if we set up our own business.

Later, we'll explore, more extensively, the generational differences and how to transform to the Type T leader, while including all generations in the process. But the bottom line is that Living The New Normal is unlike anything we have ever seen or experienced before. And the leader of the future will not look like the leaders of the past.

Many of us cut our teeth in business under leaders who exercised the "command and control" style of management. This is the quintessential Type A leadership style. It's more of a traditional military style, where the commander commanded and the soldiers followed. There were strict protocols to be followed, and people were expected to be "good soldiers. That approach worked fine as long as we had a draft system for the military, and the majority of men were required to enlist for service. But when the draft was eliminated and women started entering the workforce and the military in professional and leadership level positions, the rules of the management game started to change.

In the 1970's, after the draft was eliminated and the Viet Nam war ended, many of the traditional Ivy League schools started admitting women. The Women's Movement was making waves and more women were making "non-traditional" education and career choices. Doors were opening and women were entering careers other than nursing and teaching. All of these changes would eventually have a big impact and formulate the characteristics of the Millennial generation, which will be addressed specifically in Chapter 17.

So fast-forward from the 1970's and 1980's to the late 1990's and the 21st century. Women are in more leadership roles than ever before—if not at the CEO level, certainly in the management ranks. During this time, many of the women adopted the behaviors of the Type A "power" leader to survive and, in many cases, excelled and were promoted to the next levels of leadership. It was also during this time that MBAs were entering the workforce in record numbers. Having an MBA was required in many organizations. It was like Gordon Gekko's famous statement in the 1987 movie *Wall Street,* "Greed is good" became the unspoken, but acceptable mantra. All eyes were on the bottom line. All eyes were on quarterly earnings. Decisions were being made to make the bottom line look good to drive up stock prices. While some firms attempted to do long-range planning, decisions were being made for the short-term financial gain. Unspoken short-cuts in product quality and safety were de rigeur.

Then a funny thing happened in the 2000's . . .

Many of the women who had been on the rise in corporate leadership during this time started to become empty nesters. Many had probably advanced to the highest level in the organization they were going to achieve. At about the same time, menopause and all the hormonal and attitudinal shifts that occur during this time were unfolding too. Then, it seems like all of a sudden, women hit the brakes and started thinking "This is it? I've worked my &%^$ off for this? I don't think I can do this anymore."

And so begins the process of becoming a Type T leader. Just as the analogy of the snake shedding its skin, many women in the organizational management ranks start to shed the trappings of the way things have been done. Whether it's changes in family or organizational structure, internal mental or physical changes or all of them combined, many women want to set themselves free.

As stated earlier, many men also experience a shift in their leadership attitude, often in their mid-50s and 60's. Maybe the catalyst is a health issue that prompts concerns about mortality and their legacy. They begin to question if they want their legacy to be based on their contribution to a strong bottom line. Many would rather focus on broader community or global issues and making the world a better place for their grandchildren.

Freedom to Be Intentional—My Story and Reinvention

One of the great things about getting older is that we have the capacity to look back, knowing what we know now and have learned over the course of twenty or thirty or even forty years. While we each have changed and the world is, admittedly, markedly different, there are many things that have remained the same. The key is to determine what has worked well for you in the past and how to adapt or modify it, if necessary, for the 21st century.

For example, most of my career I was a human resources executive. When I left my last corporate position in late 1999, the world was on the cusp of significant technological changes, which gave rise to a plethora of new kinds of work over the next decade. In addition, there were lifestyle changes due to Baby Boomers becoming empty nesters and after September 11, 2001, there were significant downsizings in large corporations. Hundreds of thousands of people were laid off during the first decade of the new millennium.

Traditional jobs, lifestyles and career goals and direction were turned upside down when we look back more than a decade.

But at the time, of course, I didn't know how all these changes would impact our world, as we knew it. I was just eager to redefine and reshape my career, doing what I did best in new formats, outside of the corporate structure. It may well be a combination of external events and personal growth that creates your desire and motivation to change. For me, and I would guess for many others, the catalyst was more of a personal redefinition.

So in 1999, forging my own new path, I started with what I did best. I knew I was good at developing and training people. I was good at helping people and organizations lead and manage change. At the time, after 20 years in a corporate environment, I didn't want to be a human resources consultant, which was one of the few known options at the time. But I had heard about a new field called "life coaching," and a year or two later "business coaching" emerged. So in 1999, I was certified as a life coach. I took a new ventures course and did a feasibility study to see if I could make a living doing this. After running the numbers and projections, it looked like it would work. The course instructors were leery. They'd never heard of such a thing, despite the fact that life and business coaches had been in business on the East and West coasts for a couple years already. Regardless, my new venture was off and running—doing what I did best and enjoying every minute of it.

But I missed the business world, so I started by buying a business coaching franchise, one of the first in the country. This venture involved a significant financial investment and extensive training. Within three months, the tragedy of September 11 occurred and, needless to say, the bottom fell out from under me, and I lost everything—except the knowledge gained.

I share this story with you because as you define your new vision and purpose, most likely you will be building on what you do best. The trendy term now is "repurposing." You will be repurposing your skills, repackaging them to meet contemporary needs. Whatever obstacles you find along the way, you will still be going after what is truly satisfying and fits your skills, even if the "look" or path to it changes.

In the years since 1999, my work has morphed into different renditions of life and business coaching. It's been redefined several times, and the delivery methods have changed to meet the needs of businesses and to the changing economy. National speaking and consulting on organizational change have been the predominant focus for over five years now. But the essence is still the same, and my key words have been my guide for 15 years: empowering, regenerating, sustainable. Empowering people with knowledge, skills, tools and resources so that it can be regenerated in their environment and be sustainable—providing all the necessary training, facilitation, coaching and consulting guidance whether I am there or not.

To Be or Not to Be an Entrepreneur

As you embark on redefining and repurposing the skills for your new vision, it's important to know where you want to make a difference. For example, are you most comfortable in large corporations? Or do you prefer smaller or more entrepreneurial settings? Not for profit? Associations? Family owned? Publicly traded?

Are you interested or have the stamina to start your own business? Because Type T leadership in being a solo entrepreneur has some additional needs and requirements, the appendix has some information devoted to this endeavor, when you are a one-person show. You will have clients and possibly subcontractors—Type T leadership still applies and will still produce personal and financial benefits.

The kinds of environments that you enjoyed the most and that worked best for you in the past will be a good indicator of future success. Following your instincts and trusting yourself regarding the best organizational fit is critical.

Finding an Organizational Fit

My recommendation is that, for most people, finding the right fit in another organization is probably the best choice to start raising the bar on their contribution to a higher level of leadership.

It's essential to be clear about what worked best for you in the past, in terms of organization size, level of autonomy, industries that are a good fit, location etc.

Just as you created your list of key words of who you want to be as a leader, it's a good idea to create a list of the elements that you want in your next environment that will encourage and facilitate the ability for you to fully contribute.

Be thorough, as I have seen people create masterful lists of what they want in their next organizational leadership position only to miss a key point that eventually derailed their ability to fully contribute. See my client Sarah's list below as an example:

- Salary of $150,000 or more.
- Executive position, reporting to the president.
- For-profit, entrepreneurial environment.
- Well known and respected in the industry.
- Good company values and solid financial reputation.
- Opportunity to use her skills to make a difference.

There were more things on the list, and she got almost all of them. On the surface, it appeared to be her dream job—until she learned that her colleagues and co-executives didn't support her function or want her in that role. They wanted someone else. After a while, she was stonewalled every step of the way.

The missing items on the list were "Budgetary and organizational support for the position, the function and ME!" During her three years at the company, she did her best to contribute to the organizational goals, using her Type T leadership skills in a bottom-line world. She saw the handwriting on the wall, and she actually trained her replacement —the person they wanted in the job all along, but who wasn't ready for the position when she was hired. Her position was eliminated during a restructuring, and she received a nice severance package, which afforded her to pursue her true dream job—as an entrepreneur.

Another client thought he could easily transition from being a vice president in the for-profit world to being an executive director in the not-for-profit sector. It didn't take long before he saw the differences in mindsets, priorities and decision-making criteria between the for-profit community and the not-for-profit community. It drove him crazy. They were not "his people." He felt like a fish out of water; he struggled with the board's expectations and with his constituents' demands and desires. ✒

So, in summary, as you embark on defining your new vision and purpose, it's critically important to spend time and reflection on the following:

- Knowing what you do best.
- Knowing the environments that are best for you.
- Exploring the cultures of various organizations to see if they could be a good fit.
- Examining how you can "repurpose" your skills.
- Determining if you need to update or learn new skills to be contemporary.

One final note on how to determine what you do best. All of my clients who are making career changes are encouraged, and often required, to get the book *StrengthsFinders 2.0* by Tom Rath. Believe it or not, this is not a book you have to read! But you do have to buy it to obtain an access code to take an online assessment, which will provide a personalized report of your top five strengths.

This assessment is one of the best I've seen and truly summarizes the key strengths for each executive I've coached. We have incorporated their strengths in their resumes, providing examples of the strengths based on actual work experiences.

As you embark on finding the right place, you'll have a new tool to concisely express what you do best and prove how you've utilized those skills in the past.

Characteristics
of Type T Leadership

Chapter 8

Type T's Take a Holistic Point of View

Sharing the Vision

As stated earlier, most people will choose to contribute their skills in an organizational setting. Some may stay with their current employer. Some may change employers, seeking a better alignment with their values, and some may make a greater shift by seeking opportunities in the not-for-profit arena or dedicate themselves to volunteer leadership, community boards or political activities.

Regardless of which avenue you pursue, the concepts of implementing Type T leadership can be applied in any setting.

It starts with taking time to share the vision. The vision may be about the company as a whole and/or it may be for the areas over which you have oversight. The part that distinguishes you, as a Type T leader, from the others is in how you share the vision. It's not a yearly event. It's not handing out the annual report or sending voluminous packets of information to employees' homes to show the family members you care.

Sharing the vision is a personal investment of your time and energy with your staff and colleagues. It's about translating the vision for the company into group and personal initiatives. It's about taking that corporate vision and translating it, so each department is part of the whole and contributes to the success of the organization. And, it's about making it come alive in the minds and hearts of your team.

One of the best ways to start is to focus on your team leaders and make sure they are not only informed but are part of the process of how to make the vision come alive for their teams. This is best done in a specially planned team building session. If possible, an offsite meeting place would be ideal to allow for more creativity. During this time, you'll explain the "why." Why it's important to have a vision, why your vision is intended to be a catalyst, how they fit into the vision and the process for employee engagement.

Later we'll walk through the whole process of creating the vision in more detail, but for now, all you need to know is that as you discover and start to implement your higher purpose of leadership and live in true authenticity, it all starts with your vision for the future.

In the past you probably set expectations with your team and held them accountable and that will continue. However, the bar has now been raised for you, as well as your team when the new vision is created.

Since you've started your own path of higher accountability and authenticity, you'll be introducing the concept to your team of truly being accountable for the results they produce. You will want to share the Get Out of B.E.D. model with them because you and your team will be raising the level of integrity for how you operate, how you communicate and how you produce results. Sloppy service will no longer be tolerated. Bad behaviors will not be ignored. Finger pointing and blaming of other people or departments for slip-ups will start to be a thing of the past. Nothing will change until, collectively, the group is more aware and conscious of being accountable, taking ownership of the vision and contributing to the implementation.

The transformational leader is one who leads with accountability and integrity. Anything less will be out of alignment of who you know yourself to be. Again, courage will be essential. And you cannot expect perfection. Because, as a Type T leader, you know this is a process. You know that any mistakes that happen are learning opportunities or provide the opportunity to reinforce, clarify or explain the vision and its purpose with your team.

As you and your team practice higher levels of accountability, not only are your expectations of your team shifted and elevated, but what and how you delegate will change as well. Delegation and coaching are the keys to the development of future leaders and the Type T leader knows and embraces this process. The Type A leaders are very busy making sure they are the experts, they are the ones who want to be in charge and they are the ones who receive all the recognition. This is no longer you.

Transformational leaders include others in the process, share the power and provide recognition as it is earned. Note that it must be "earned." There is a big difference between a leader who holds people accountable and one who abdicates accountability and responsibility. Type A leaders may abdicate responsibility by delegating tasks they don't want to handle or tasks that have low visibility. Whereas, Type T leaders understand that these tasks may provide just the right learning points for their direct reports that will stretch their skills and provide a chance for them to test the waters of greater responsibility in a safe environment and under their coaching and guidance.

The next distinction of how Type T leaders guide others is in the action plans they create. At this point, your action plans will include longer-term intentions for personal and professional development, as well as specific action plans for the department and teams who are instrumental in achieving the vision.

Your intentions for your own development are important because you need to stay on top of your game. The focus of development and your action plans for your continued growth will probably shift from industry-specific learning and seminars to books or seminars that address more holistic ways of thinking and being. You may be drawn to books on health and wellness, spirituality, the arts or sciences that will help you grow and expand your dimensions as a leader. Successful Type T leaders often draw on very disparate sources of information to achieve new results.

Another form of action plans that may emerge can be in the form of being an industry thought-leader. Instead of attending conferences to build skills, this may be a time to submit proposals to speak at industry conferences. You are being sought out as more of a visionary leader, to share wisdom and provide thought-provoking insights to raise awareness and challenge others. The egocentric Type A leader sees these experiences as "Look at me! I've made it!" experiences. The Type T leader sees the opportunity to contribute to others. It goes from "all about me" to "all about you."

In turn, you will start to pay attention and discuss your direct reports' developmental action plans in greater detail and with more frequency. Their involvement is critical for buy-in and commitment.

Action plans will be about them—not you. Understanding their goals and motivations will be essential.

I recall two star players on my team many years ago, who had dramatically different personal and professional goals. Being part of their development was very exciting.

Diane was an assistant director and mom with two young children. I remember her advising me that she would give me 100+% at work every day, eight to five, five days a week. When necessary, she would work overtime to achieve results as needed. But she was very clear that she would not be working overtime on a regular basis, and she would not be available or striving for "face time" at all hours of the day. She was my right-hand person, and I respected her choices. And she did provide 100+% every day. I couldn't, and didn't, ask for more because higher levels of leadership were not a priority for her. Being of service, producing high quality work and being a great mom and wife were her priorities.

Chris, on the other hand was a gritty and edgy, diamond-in-the-rough supervisor who had big dreams. She was tough and wanted to prove herself if given the chance. A teenage bride and divorced at 22, there was a lot of baseline work to do to establish credibility. Upon reflection, she was probably an Aspiring Type A supervisor, who was dependent upon bosses for information and support. She was striving to be a Type A with all her might! My job was to help her get there.

We started with her appearance. She had a tendency to dress like she was leaving work to go "clubbing" or bar hopping. At the time, a tailored, conservative business suit was more appropriate. No low-cut blouses and sexy hair, and she had to spit out the gum. She had to start thinking of herself as a leader.

Next she had to start speaking like a leader. No more double negatives, ain'ts and swear words. We worked on grammar 101. She enrolled in college and started working on her degree. Chris was the first person in her family to go to school beyond high school.

We worked on some high profile projects. Each step along the way we would discuss the steps needed, why a particular action would be best and how to communicate it. We would rehearse and practice her presentations before going before leadership groups with program or project implementation. She was a sponge, and it was thrilling to watch her grow.

While I had lost track of Chris after leaving the organization, I learned that she married a prominent lawyer in the community and became a high-level executive at the company where we worked together. It still makes me proud to have been part of her transformation.

Type T Leaders Think Holistically

It also is not uncommon for Type T's to be sought out by people from other departments and organizations for mentoring or coaching. People trust the authenticity and sense a level of integrity that is not present with so many other leaders.

So how, specifically, does a contemporary leader think? And how is it different from other leaders?

First, transformational leaders who are driven to lead with a higher purpose take a holistic approach to inquiries and decision-making. What this means is that you start by looking at whole systems, rather than starting with analysis of the individual parts. Some people might call this "big picture" thinking. However, I have known a lot of people who can grasp the big picture but lack the capacity, interest or attention to detail to consider the impact and influence on all the parts that make up the whole. A transformational leader understands that the whole is only as good as the summation of the parts. You might say effective, contemporary leaders use a whole-part-whole thinking process. In this case, you would take a strategic approach to the whole system that is under review or consideration. During this process, you involve others who have an interest and capacity for big picture ideas.

The next phase is to involve people who are knowledgeable about the parts that make up the whole. This would mean involving individuals who have functional responsibility for operations, IT, HR, finance, sales, legal or any other area that would be impacted by the strategic plan. During this phase, the functional managers or team leaders are tasked to review the process to determine the impact and how to implement the new procedure or process.

Your job is to hold the vision of the bigger plan in mind and see how to make it work or raise the flag when there are issues that can be potential problems. Their job is to consider not just their area, function or department, but to collaborate with colleagues to follow the flow of the process to assure smooth transitions along the way.

Findings and recommendations are then brought back for review to see if they meet or excede the goals of the strategic plan.

The common thread throughout the process is that the intent is always that the end result will be in the best interest or for the good of the whole. Team members at every stage must be on the same wavelength regarding this philosophy. To ensure this will happen, you serve as a champion or sponsor to coach, guide and facilitate the process—always holding the big picture or vision as the benchmark.

This last step is one where traditional leaders frequently fail. They may be the champion or sponsor in name only and are reluctant to shepherd the project and the people through a higher-level thought process.

This higher-level thought process encourages all of the players to be of service and look out for the good of the whole. It means being of service and looking out for the best interests of:

- Employees.
- Customers.
- Shareholders.
- Vendors and suppliers.
- Board members.
- The communities in which you operate.

There is no room for hidden agendas or self-serving interests.

At this point, you may be thinking, "This is going to be really hard. People in organizations won't buy into this." It may sound a little naïve, but I can assure you that some of the most successful companies in America today are incorporating many of these concepts.

Again, it's the intention to strive for this approach. Because, if for no other reason, taking a holistic, collaborative approach will be better for your heath, as we saw in Chapter 3.

So how do contemporary leaders talk? How do they communicate so that people follow?

First and foremost, Type T leaders listen. They listen to content and listen for context. They listen to intent. They listen for impact and the emotion behind the words. They listen to thoughts plus feelings to get the whole meaning.

One of my clients had a tendency to be abrupt and considered employee one-on-one or team meetings to be a waste of time because, as she said, "No one talks."

There was a good reason no one talked. She didn't listen. And, she didn't care what they had to say. She just wanted them to produce results.

She made an observation that I thought was quite interesting. She said that when she interviewed people for a job, she was really thorough in asking questions and getting to know the applicants to see if they were a good fit—i.e if they make her job easier. Her interview questions were about meeting her needs. Somehow, after they were hired, she stopped listening to them because she expected them to continue to meet her needs. After all, that's what they were hired for.

As she learned and practiced new listening skills in her one-on-one sessions with employees, she found that not only did she learn about them as individuals and their motivations, but their productivity increased, and they started contributing in team meetings about ways to improve processes. Her one-on-ones and team meetings were no longer about her; the focus was more about them, the team, the department and the bigger picture.

This, very simply, is employee engagement.

Contemporary leaders understand engagement. They listen and they collaborate.

The communication style of a Type T leader is more facilitation. They facilitate discussions to achieve consensus and collaboration. Type A's, on the other hand, are informers, rather than facilitators.

You cannot have the intention to "look out for the good of the whole," if you're not willing to collaborate.

Collaboration and Giving Up the Need to Be Right

During a trip to rural Kenya, I had the opportunity to meet and spend time with the local community leaders. Rural Kenyans are part of a group society. They make decisions based on community needs. I heard countless examples of how they collaborated on very complex issues, sometimes involving over 500 people. One example involved how profits from sales at the local market would be used. In essence, they had a combination of a co-op and a bank, since government banks had interest rates over 25-30%. They would pool crops or goods and sell them at the market. There were elections for community leaders, who would determine who got loans and how profits would be dispersed.

They always had the intention of looking out for the good of the whole. When asked what they would do if a person had his or her own agenda or were resistant, they responded, "We just keep talking." It's important to note that what they talked about was the vision, the goals and the benefits for the community. In essence, the leaders kept the "big picture" alive for the community. They also have a unique object called a Rungu or Blessing Stick that is present during group meetings. Unlike the Rungu that is a weapon, the Blessing Stick is a beaded wooden baton used by respected village elders in community gatherings and meetings. It represents status, authority and wisdom. My understanding is that if a person were being selfish and self-serving, the Blessing Stick would be passed to them to hold until they could collaborate for the good of the whole. It was a symbolic gesture that pointed out that the individual's behavior was inconsistent with community goals.

I think every organization should have a Blessing Stick!

Another element of effective collaboration is giving up the need to be right. If you're positional and steadfast in your approach, it can provide very little room for negotiation or collaboration. In essence, when you insist on being right, it makes the other person wrong— and it is contrary to the accountability/ Get Out of B.E.D. model.

In summary, Type T leaders understand the importance of keeping the vision and collaboration present and alive. They are also aware of the opportunities to reinforce the concepts and applications of it. For example, they will recognize the accomplishment of small steps that lead to the bigger picture, as a reminder of how each piece and part is integral to overall success. This reinforces employee engagement. It acknowledges teams and individuals for their contribution to the greater whole.

This is particularly important when the implementation of a project can take many months or years. For example, each month when I met with the client who was working on shifting corporate culture, we would review progress and steps taken. Since it was a yearlong contract, each month we looked at where we started, and the team would share their perspectives on what was going well and how things had improved. At the end of my consulting engagement, while more work was needed and the process wasn't complete by any means, the funding had run out. So, at the "completion ceremony," we spent time debriefing in more detail. The members of the team were asked to describe the environment and culture when we started. They described how they used to communicate with each other, what it was like and all the steps that then led to a more cohesive, collaborative group. One person said, "I can't believe we used to act that way!"

It was through subtle shifts in thinking, taking ownership and accountability in particular, that they were able to make some quantum leaps.

While we would have liked to continue having me involved on a regular basis, the funding only permitted two or three times a year for "check ups." However, the goal was always to empower the team with knowledge, skills, tools and resources so that it would be regenerating, shared and passed on to others so it could be sustained. They knew the vision of the culture they wanted to create, and they had the tools and skills to keep it in place. As long as they stayed accountable, it would work!

Chapter 9

Unraveling the Myths and Mysteries of Power

Remembering Our Rise to Power

For some reason, as people advance in their careers, there's a hesitation when it comes to owning their power. "Absolute power corrupts absolutely!" Powerful people are often feared. We hear more often about the abuses of power than its benevolence.

Yet, I think many people aspire to positions of power, despite all the negative connotations. We start our career, wide-eyed and wanting to make a difference, to be different from those who preceded us. Youthful idealism, some would say.

I don't really think that people set out to use their power abusively. But somewhere, somehow along the way, they may lose sight of the vision or the dream of making a difference and succumb to the trappings associated with power. The wealth, the influence, the status, the perks. And, eventually, it becomes more about influencing others to do things that may ultimately be self-serving. If we think about political leaders, corporate executives and, in particular, world leaders, there's a heightened awareness, thanks to the media, of the wrongdoings of people in positions of power or leadership.

But, if we reflect on our own careers and how we rose to positions of power, influence and leadership, it can be easy to see how these abuses could have occurred or how we might have lost sight of our original intentions. I have seen how having power in organizations can become a heady experience, as we rise in our levels of responsibility and are rewarded in many visible and tangible ways. To start, it's important to look at how aspiring or emerging Type A leaders might use power to get a sense of their starting point. It will also help to understand not only the Type A approach to power, but help clarify the transition to and differences between Type A and Type T leaders and their relationship or perspective of power.

Aspiring Type A—Learning the Ropes? Earning Stripes?

For many of us, we started our careers at a much lower level of power and influence. We really hadn't earned our stripes, and we were the "wannabes." Hagberg called this a Stage 2 characteristic—power by association. While not all people demonstrating Stage 2 characteristics want to take on greater roles and responsibilities in an organization, these are often the characteristics of an *aspiring* Type A. Remember, Type A has traditionally been the exalted model of leadership and the one that is represented most often in advertising and media. And as aspiring Type A's, we wanted a piece of the action! We did everything we could to earn the title or work on visible projects, and we might have been a bit manipulative. There's a level of what I call "professional immaturity." Does any of this sound familiar? At this point in your "power career," you don't know what you don't know. There can be loftiness about being an organizational leader, like there's a certain magic that comes with the position. Glenda the Good Witch with her wand and poof! Suddenly, you're the great decider and influencer.

Frequently, the Aspiring Type A person can be heard saying, "I could do that!" despite no experience or capacity. I remember, and now laugh at, my own thoughts when I was an Aspiring Type A. I used to say: "I think that I can be a great leader and make good organizational decisions, if I have the right information." Duh. Who wouldn't! What I didn't realize then is that leaders often don't have the right, complete or accurate information to make decisions. It could be that there are a lot of unknowns and only through time will more information emerge or there may be organizational drones who may filter, slant and withhold information to sabotage a leader.

So starting out as an Aspiring Type A is where we learn the ropes, and, hopefully, we've had good mentors along the way. There's a reliance on people who we see as a mentor or guide at this point and often there is a starry-eyed view of them, as if they can do no wrong. Then, if and when that person falls off the pedestal, it can be quite a jolt and disconcerting. That may be one of the first wake-up calls or "crisis" to growing and advancing to a higher approach to leadership because, at this point, we have to learn how to stand on our own and not in the shadows of our heroes.

Remembering what it was like for us as we advanced in our responsibilities will be important when we think about how to use our power positively as an authentic, transformational leader. As Type T leaders, we are now mentoring, coaching and guiding people in their careers, and we want to do it "right!" This is a very different approach from the Aspiring Type A and the Type A leaders.

Power and the Type A Leader

Remember that first promotion to a supervisory position? Welcome to the start of Type A power. Think back to how you felt with that new title, the business cards, attending a conference or professional development program. I remember being so excited to attend my first professional development program, a week-long, specialized workshop held at a major university. I stayed at a "conference facility" on campus—just for the attendees—which turned out to be a glorified dormitory. But so what? I was a "professional" now.

The glow of this opportunity was diminished, however, when I learned that my mentor made a career of jetting to fancy places, staying at fancy hotels and eating at fancy restaurants—not like the dorm and cafeteria food I experienced. I also learned that, despite all of my mentor's glamorous trips, there was little return on investment for the organization in terms of applying or implementing anything of substance to improve it. She was eventually "encouraged" to pursue other opportunities, and I was left to figure out how to take what I had learned from her, make it my own and show a good return on any investment made in my professional development. It was extremely disappointing to realize that this person, who had been my mentor and who I had tremendously admired, had abused the power that she had.

And, I also remember the opportunities that came with this new position and how growing into that Type A powerbroker was pretty cool. It was the "LOOK AT ME!" phenomenon as discussed in earlier chapters—very egocentric and a fair amount of "chest pounding" to show off accomplishments, all the while trying to do so without looking too obnoxious. It's just that we're so proud of ourselves for the things we know, the people we hang out with, the things we get to do, the things we get to buy, the influence we get to display . . . and on and on and on.

There's an expression that Type A leaders may use to show they're committed to using their power to impact the bottom line: "I'm taking names and kicking butt!"

The media thrives on appealing to people who are Type A leaders. This is the pinnacle of success. The watches you wear, the cars you buy, the shoes that make the right statement of your status and taste. Even what you drink—be it water, wine or whiskey. The media also influences how you spend your free time, where you travel, what your home is like and the recreational activities that you choose. Type A leaders are image-conscious, and the media helps shape that image of "success" so you can look the part and feel successful.

In addition to the status of material goods, Type A's are often going to be very deliberate about being seen in all the right places with all the right people. Casually, or not so casually, dropping names of people at the trendy event or fundraisers. Posting "selfies" on Facebook at the hip restaurants or concerts. These people don't post many pictures on Facebook of others, particularly those who aren't cool or well known or any place that isn't considered to be trendy.

The important thing about this is not that it's bad to want recognition or to look good or to hang out with cool people. For lack of a better expression—it just is what it is, not good or bad. It's just part of this leadership development process.

Again, your power as a Type A leader is a lot about looking good. It may seem at the outset like you're being benevolent or empowering, but the bottom line is that you want to be recognized for your good deeds, expertise or "having it all." Your humble statement: "No really, I couldn't have done it without all of you…" may contain all the right words, but it's still all about you.

Until, that is, you find yourself starting to feel uncomfortable with all this "stuff." That's when you think, "I must be crazy." I've worked so hard for this, and everyone says and thinks I'm successful, and this is what success looks like. What's wrong with me?

The Transition Period

In my experience, I completely agree with Hagberg, who says there's usually a crisis of some kind that takes place before moving to the next stage of power. For example, seeing your mentor and hero abuse their role, as I did, or increased responsibilities can be a catalyst to those who have previously relied heavily on others' guidance and support to bolster their success.

We've talked before about how a personal or professional crisis can precipitate a major shift in thinking, particularly after being so successful as a Type A leader.

Personal changes such as a divorce, death or illness of a family member or close friend may be the wake-up call that prompts you to take action in a new direction. These life changes can, and will, test your assumptions about who you know yourself to be, the choices that you have made in the past and want to make in the future.

Organizational change may be the impetus that creates the crisis. Mergers, acquisitions, restructuring, downsizing, changes in leadership and loss of your job are classic examples that can prompt a person to step back and do a forced reflection about what's important.

These kinds of changes, whether personal or professional, frequently result in a very real identity crisis. All of the perceived stability of previous roles, responsibilities, power and influence has been turned upside down. When you walk past the mirror, you might ask yourself, "Who is this person looking back at me? Do I know you?"

Again, all I can tell you is that this is normal. You're not crazy.

Now that you've come to grips with the past perceptions of power, the inevitable losses associated with the changes and realization that you're ready for something new, we can start creating your new, transformational power base and begin using your power positively, deliberately and intentionally!

Using Your Power Positively

Weaving together the concepts and practices discussed so far, we'll apply them in a new way as they relate to the positive use of your power.

One of the first steps will be to write down all your current perceptions of power. Make a detailed list and describe:

- How you currently use your power.
- The ways that you think you demonstrate power.
- How you feel about using your power.
- How you feel when others exercise power with or *over* you.
- What having power means to you.
- What it feel like to be questioning it all.

Next, review the Get Out of B.E.D. model and take a realistic look at your perceptions and comments and determine if you're following O.A.R and T.W.A.—ownership, accountability and responsibility for your thoughts, words and actions *related* to power. Are you a victim to other people's power? Or do you feel courageous and victorious in your perceptions and actions related to your own power?

Remember, using power is a choice, and you get to choose when and how you exercise your power with yourself and with others.

Type T Power

So what does Type T power look and sound like?

In my opinion, this is the heart of authentic leadership because it's not about you, but about being of service to others, empowering and recognizing them. It is an intentional approach to developing and acknowledging, to being a resource to others, so they are not dependent upon you and yet make decisions and choices that are also for the good of the whole.

The Type T leader is committed to grooming and transferring ownership to others, staying in the background to support and assist when needed.

Here are the ways that you can start that process with your team. Keep in mind that these concepts can be applied to direct reports, volunteer teams and even family members. One caveat is that you must have permission to coach or have an agreement to coach another person first. There is nothing worse than to try to coach someone who doesn't want your guidance, particularly if you are not his or her supervisor or you are not an expert or qualified to provide guidance or feedback for improvement.

So let's start with the teams or groups of people you oversee, who are responsible for producing some kind of results, whether at work or for a volunteer organization.

Using your power positively, you start by discussing the team's role and how it relates to the organization's vision and mission. People need to have context and a clear picture of how they fit in with the whole. What is their purpose in this process? Having a clear understanding of roles and responsibilities is the basis for establishing expectations and setting goals.

What I am describing here may sound like the basic supervisory skills that you learned 20 or 30 years ago. But I can assure you that the Type T leader who is raising the bar to a higher purpose of leadership is approaching this process very differently.

For the Type A leader, it is more *transactional* than transformational. Review job description–check! Tell them what you want and expect—check! Tell them their goals—another check! And done. Then three, six or twelve months later, Type A leaders might sit down with their direct reports and talk about how they're doing. Oftentimes their feedback is mostly about what they did wrong. Their approach is formulaic and much like that checklist to be completed.

How do I know? Early in my career, I was promoted to a new position and tasked with starting a training department. I remember the conversation clearly: My Type A boss said the company was going to double in size in three years (from 500 to 1000 employees). Continued excellent customer service was essential, and we needed to have people ready to assume supervisory and management positions. He wanted me to start a new training department, but there wasn't a budget for it . . . and there was no place or room to do training . . .and he said that while he had confidence in me, other leaders weren't really sure if it would work or if I were the right person. So, they'd give me a small raise and see how it went in six months. Oh yeah, then there was the huge list of things to accomplish by then . . .

This list had about 15 things to accomplish in that short, six-month period. First and foremost was to create customer service training programs and a professional development course for supervisors.

Being the eager, new Type A leader, I was ecstatic to prove myself and willingly jumped in, guns a-blazing to show them what I could do. Raise or no raise.

After conducting a needs analysis with managers, I created beginning and advanced customer service classes, recruited the best customer service people in the company and trained them to teach the classes. Since there was no room for training, I negotiated with the facilities manager to convert two coat closets to training rooms, which could each accommodate 12 people. They even put in ventilation! More than 50 people attended classes in my first six months on the job, and the programs were really well received.

I created a three-day supervisory course on listening and negotiation skills. Thirty people attended two off-site programs that I facilitated, which were wildly successful, much to the amazement of the senior management.

The day for my six-month review finally arrived. To say I was proud is an understatement. Not only had I delivered on the two most important goals, but they had exceeded everyone's expectations.

My boss, who I idolized and really wanted to please, said I did a good job, but that I didn't meet all of the goals and expectations.

WHAT??? *^&^$^#%@Q

He then pointed to a couple low-level priorities at the bottom of the list.

I reminded him of all that had been accomplished through my Herculean (Type A) efforts, which he did not deny. But then he said, "You agreed to accomplish all 15 items, not just a couple. So, I can only give you a 'meets expectations' rating."

To close the loop on that story, I learned several valuable lessons:

- Be careful what you agree to when setting performance expectations.
- Keep your boss informed all along the way about whether goals can be met.
- Reprioritize or renegotiate expectations if it appears that the goals that were established and agreed to cannot be

reasonably achieved (I learned this the hard way by teaching the negotiation course!)

The purpose for sharing this sad story? In retrospect, I learned that a transformational leader guides the process so there are no surprises and is willing to adapt and modify to meet changing conditions or circumstances. I was working for a Type A leader who wanted to exert his power. I also learned later that he took credit for the work that I had done. Despite being deflated and ticked off, I set off to prove myself again, but this time with a slightly different leadership style.

The bottom line *after* changes in my leadership style? Over the course of the next six years, the company didn't double in size—it tripled! Over 200 volunteer trainers provided training to coworkers for 100 different training programs, and the training department received national recognition. And, I was promoted to be an officer of the company. We also created a corporate wellness program in the same way, by starting at a grass-roots level and creating employee ownership and empowerment in the process. By the time I left the company, the wellness department had a small specialized staff and over 100 employee volunteers who taught over 15 different aerobics classes and staffed a 30,000 square foot fitness facility, aerobics studio and sports park. Through collective efforts and commitment, we became one of the top 25 corporate wellness programs in the country and were ranked with Fortune 100 companies for our innovation and cost effectiveness.

I grew a lot in that process and would like to think that I always used my power effectively. But I'm sure there were many times I didn't. Clearly, a lot of good things can happen at the transitional level, as not all of aspects of Type A leadership are bad or ineffective. In fact, it can often be very effective; it's just that full-on Type T is even more so. I can't imagine how well it would have gone had I been a "fully functioning" Type T leader. But, a more complete transformation to Type T came later, and it can often feel like it is an ongoing process.

One thing I know is that real power is empowering. It's being clear about your personal vision, as well as your vision for your department or group and putting the right structures in place to lead your team. Real power is communicating goals and providing timely feedback that will be reflective of the new personal vision and purpose. Real power is having conversations that are more transformational than transactional, more empowering than factual, more empathetic and of-service than having your personal expectations met. That's real power and Type T leadership.

Chapter 10

Giving Up Fear, Old Patterns and the Need to Be Right

Fear and False Assumptions

Transformational leadership comes from within, so to create effective Type T communication, it's necessary to do a serious look inside, identifying and eliminating assumptions that get in the way of true collaborative communication.

So often during difficult times, we think that others are out to get us. We can feel like the victim and think others may want to hurt us, embarrass us, make us look bad. I'm going to suggest that if you find yourself feeling this way, that you step back, with your eyes wide open, and consider that fear may be the source of your reactions on all fronts. The colleagues that you may suspect of being out to get you may be operating out of a fear of their own, which then triggers a fear in you, which then spirals down to a mess of false assumptions. Remember that *fear* is really: False Expectations Appearing Real.

That's why I love and frequently refer to the book *The Four Agreements* by Don Miguel Ruiz. The third agreement is "Don't Make Assumptions." Ruiz says, "Find the courage to ask questions and to express what you really want. Communicate with others as clearly as you can to avoid misunderstandings, sadness and drama. With just this one agreement, you can completely transform your life."

How would your life be different if you could practice and apply just this one agreement?

Fear creates misunderstandings. Fear creates sadness—for others and ourselves. And fear creates drama, which always ends up with Blame, Excuses and Denial.

Learning how to trust your authentic self may include asking yourself the tough questions when faced with fear or making assumptions about a situation or other people.

I remember an encounter with a person close to me that had spiraled downhill. My feelings were hurt, and I was angry at his response. In the past, I would have immediately come back with snarky, passive-aggressive comments. I had a created a series of possible responses, and each one of them would have ended in a horrible escalation of the problem and misunderstanding. I wanted to be right, and I wanted to make him wrong. I wanted him to "pay" for being insensitive to my concerns.

And while I may not have liked the response he gave me, I had to remember two things. One, was he really trying to hurt me and trying to be insensitive? No. And would my past ways of replying be representative of operating out of love, collaboration and trust? No.

So then I had some choices. How important was it to me to make him wrong for being insensitive? What would I say or how would I respond if I were being loving, collaborative and trusting?

You see, sometimes, you don't necessarily have to like or agree with someone else's behavior to be true to your intentions. In this case, for me, it was more important not to make assumptions and to know that I could trust myself and trust him. I was also not committed to continuing old patterns of being snarky and passive aggressive to win a perceived argument.

I call this "knowing when to 'fold 'em.'" Just like in poker, you need to know when to put your cards down and not stay in a losing game.

And so it is in the game of collaborative communication. Staying in the game just to win or to be right won't work. Staying in the game to prove your point won't work. In the grand scheme of things, you have to be the judge of knowing what's best for the good of the whole and of staying true to your purpose and vision. You make the call.

Remember, this quest for collaborative communication is not about getting what you want. If anything, it is more about giving up the things that get in the way of true communication and true collaboration. In our world of scarcity, people cringe or fear having to give something up—even if it's unhealthy. Quitting smoking, giving up or reducing alcohol or fatty, processed foods. Giving up the comfort of our couch to go to the gym. Or, even giving up spending countless dollars on fancy coffees each day and putting that money into savings. We don't want to deny ourselves these "pleasures," although we know the healthier alternatives are better for us in the long run.

The same is true of communication. It's about giving up unhealthy patterns of communicating. At this point, I am going to pose some possibilities for you to consider. I want you to step back and observe yourself as objectively as possible. If you have done the Two Week Challenge, this process will be a little easier. But it can be painful, just the same, to see how frequently we sabotage ourselves from obtaining the very things that we want the most, such as peace of mind, love, harmony, prosperity and an abundant heart and spirit.

How often do you work to control the outcomes of interactions, decisions, choices and actions taken with your friends, family, work colleagues and/or communities? Most of us would never want to admit that we want to control others. But we do. I'm going to suggest that you're lying to yourself, if you deny the very thought that you want to control outcomes. So start by facing that fact and acknowledge that you may have a tendency to want to control others to get what you want.

The next painful realization is that you may dominate or manipulate others to get what you want. If you're resisting this thought, I want you to articulate exactly why your behaviors or actions are not dominating or manipulating—right now. Seriously. What makes you think you are not trying to dominate or manipulate outcomes to get what you want?

I guarantee that, in more cases than you might want to admit, you have found a way to rationalize or justify this behavior just to get your way.

Many people have lived these patterns for so long they no longer see them for what they are. We can dominate through logic. Pressing fact after fact on other people, when they really just want to be heard, not dictated to. We can dominate and manipulate through silence, forcing people to speculate, assume, read our minds and basically succumb to our way. And when they try to read our minds, it's never right, and they may give up, become resentful and withdraw. Then no one is happy. There are no winners.

Begin by taking ownership of what you want. Be accountable and responsible if you choose to be dominating or manipulating or controlling. Openly acknowledge it for what it is. At least there's a modicum of integrity when you acknowledge controlling behavior. It's not like you're fooling anyone or that they don't recognize when they're being manipulated.

That's what's so funny about all of this. We act like we're Harry Potter and can wear the "invisibility cloak" and pretend that no one notices our bad behavior. The truth is, they see it even when we think they don't.

I remember telling a colleague that I had changed my mind on a decision. Originally, I had said that I didn't want to interfere or influence the decision process. And after several weeks of indecision, I told the person that I had changed my mind; I did want to interfere and influence the outcome. My words were: "Maybe I changed my mind. Maybe I lied to myself and you when I said I didn't want to influence the decision. Maybe I was being selfish and wanted to get my way. But here are my thoughts for your consideration."

The reaction was some nervous laughter, a little relief and a sense of freedom for both of us that the cards were on the table. Making the decision was easier, even if it wasn't completely what I wanted. We knew, in the end, that nothing had been withheld, and it gave the other person the freedom to make a choice based on more complete information. And I felt better having come clean and forthright with my true thoughts and feelings.

Real collaboration is about giving things up that no longer serve you or others and for doing what is for the good of the whole. Giving up the need to be right is essential for real collaboration.

As a case in point, I observed a very interesting and revealing philosophical conversation between two people about the need to be right. One person said he thought the world would be a better place if people could just give up the need to be right. Amazingly, the other person pounded his fist on the table and said: "NO! What we need is more love!"

So there you have it. People unconsciously feel a basic need to be right. To my surprise, no one noticed or at least commented on the irony of this whole conversation. And believe me, I wasn't going to be the one to point it out to them!

Always be aware and notice your tendency or inclination to want to be right for the sake of being right. Acknowledge it and make a choice as to whether it's important or not.

What would happen if you gave up the need to be right? Imagine the possible outcomes. Imagine how you would feel, once the fear of the unknown subsided.

Imagine the feeling of trust, in yourself and in others, if you communicated clearly, cleanly and compassionately.

Being authentic is the way to accomplish that. It sounds so trite and "authentic" is such a trendy term. Live authentically. Authentic communication. Authentic food. Authentic happiness. Is there anyone who would actually say, "No, I prefer fake communication, and I want to live a fake life. I guess the fact that we have to make a point of using the word is evidence that a lot of people either don't know the difference between fake and genuine or are content to settle for less than the real thing.

When you live in a world of Blame, Excuses and Denial, it's hard to be authentic. When you take Ownership and Accountability and Responsibility for your thoughts, words and actions, there is a greater likelihood of authenticity.

When you're on the road to a higher level of leadership and true authenticity, you will have less tolerance for saying what is politically correct to win others over. You'll be more inclined to align your words with your head and your heart. This kind of authenticity leads to a level of vulnerability, openness and trust that people not only appreciate but know will be consistent. They connect with the vibrational energy and know that you're being authentic, even if they don't agree with you.

Living a Lie: What Can Happen When You're Out of Alignment

Remember Richard in Chapter 4, the one who blamed his staff for everything? After he worked on improved communication and had successfully built his team and shown results in his organization, he decided it was time to leave. He no longer felt aligned with the goals and direction the board had set. So he decided to leave his position and pursue something that was a better fit. It's important to note that when there is a dramatic inauthenticity in a person's life, it will permeate everything. In this case, Richard confided his big secret to me: he was gay. He'd been married, had three children and dated many women. Basically, he was living a lie. It's very hard to live in denial of who you really are and to continue that kind of balancing act for long periods of time. He lived in fear of being found out.

His inauthenticity permeated every area of his life, far beyond his sexual orientation. As he embarked on his job search, he continued to apply for positions in the medical field where he could apply the knowledge and skills that he had accumulated during the course of his career. Yet, each time he interviewed for "the perfect job," somehow he never got an offer. On paper, he was usually the perfect candidate. But during the interviews something very subtle would happen and even if he was asked back for a second interview, the job offer never came to fruition. After many months and a dwindling savings account, we had a deep heart-to-heart about why the interviews never worked out. In a very raw and vulnerable moment, he was finally honest with me and himself. He said he hated the medical field and dreaded the idea of going back into a career that he hated. BINGO! Just like Jean, who finally admitted she didn't like her colleagues, Richard's vibrational energy about not liking the medical industry seeped through. While hiring managers liked him, in the final analysis, they just didn't think he was the right fit. No wonder.

For Richard, he had become so accustomed to living a lie in his personal life that he thought that he could live a lie in his professional life, too. That was until both worlds came tumbling down upon him. As he began his transformation to a life of greater authenticity, it was no longer possible to hide his sexuality or work in an industry that was out of alignment with what brought joy and satisfaction. He could no longer accept or tolerate the fact that he lived beyond his means and hadn't paid his taxes in several years.

I'm happy to report that Richard made a career transition to a management position in the financial services industry. And while he had not shared his sexual orientation with his children or family, who lived in another state, his social life and friendships were more aligned and a better fit to his authentic life. Over time, he restored his credit rating and filed his past due taxes.

While this is a pretty dramatic example of what can happen when we lead inauthentic lives, just know that we each have areas of inauthenticity that can prevent us from reaching the higher level of leadership and influence what we desire most in our lives. It's like peeling an onion. Just when you think that you have some life or relationship issues handled, they show up in a new form to examine again.

It's learning how to trust and embrace the process that will allow us each to grow authentically and assist others in the process as well.

The bottom line to remember when it comes to collaborative communication is that it starts with you giving things up. Giving up being controlling and forcing outcomes. Giving up being right. Giving up being inauthentic. Giving up old communication patterns will be the key.

When you change how you communicate, everyone around you will change. This is just one of the many benefits of being a Type T leader.

Chapter 11

Listening to Your Inner
Voice and Intuition

If you Google "communication skills" there are literally millions of possibilities to choose from. The line in the old movie, *Cool Hand Luke,* sums up what many of us experience on a daily basis: "What we have here is a failure to communicate."

The pace and delivery methods for communication have changed dramatically in the past 30 years. We are receiving more information per second than ever before. No wonder there are communication breakdowns. And just as we talked about all of the changes since 2008, our national and global issues have become increasingly complex and often contentious. Frankly, I think it makes everyone a little bit edgy, which naturally impacts how we communicate with each other.

How do we break this edgy cycle? How do we step out of the fray and set ourselves apart if we are, in fact, taking our leadership to a higher level? How do true transformational leaders communicate differently? How do they communicate authentically?

Unconditional Listening

It starts with listening. Ironically, most people think that improving communication starts with talking. I facilitated a roundtable discussion at a large conference on how to achieve "courageous collaboration." I asked the participants why they chose this roundtable discussion and what they hoped to learn. Unanimously, their responses had to do with getting people to do what they wanted. Not exactly courageous. Not exactly collaborative. In fact, trying to get people to do what we want sounds more like manipulation than collaboration.

But that's how we are. We live in a world where people want their own way. They want this, they want that—they want things they don't really want or need. For many, the point is to exert power to get what they want.

The one thing that most people want, but don't get, is to be heard. To truly be listened to. There's a philosophy that says that if you want more of something, you should give whatever it is away. Want more money? Make a donation. Want more love? Extend love to others. It would seem that if you want to truly be heard, listening to others would be a good place to start.

Yet it's not that easy. We have been conditioned since birth that we will be listened to. The baby cries and the parent is checking to see if she's hungry or wet or has a fever. As we get older, the attentiveness diminishes, and yet, we secretly yearn to have someone tend to our needs and listen unconditionally.

We want to receive that listening but are afraid or reluctant to give it. As a result, there's a scarcity of unconditional listening. Keep in mind that unconditional listening does not imply agreement.

Listening is a skill that can be learned and like any other skill, if practiced, you can become quite adept in creating collaborative environments and achieving great results. It does require patience, with yourself and others. And you can't expect unconditional listening to be reciprocated, which can be very challenging because we want to be heard too.

By now you know the importance of aligning your thoughts, words and actions with your intentions. Hopefully you have been practicing to gain some mastery and are seeing the benefits and results of that alignment. The next step is to apply that concept to your listening in order to achieve collaborative communication.

How are you listening to other people? Are you listening through your filter or theirs? To raise your leadership to a higher level of purpose and intentionality, your listening needs to be focused on the conversation in the present moment. As you engage in conversations with the people you are mentoring or developing, and with their permission for you to give feedback, start listening to their conversations to see if their thoughts, their words and their actions are aligned with what you know to be their highest good—not yours. Since you have been practicing the art of listening to your own internal dialogue, you will be able to hear the inconsistencies or lack of alignment in others.

A coaching client of mine repeatedly talked about his desire to coach and develop his people. They read a couple of business books a month and had group discussions. He knew the theory of every model or contemporary leadership practice. I often felt like I was a part of a book club or listening to a book report when I talked to him. What was missing was the application of the concepts, in real life, in real time. He would express frustration with his managers for not being available and following up immediately when he wanted or needed information, so he would dive into the weeds and task people two or three levels down to get what he wanted, never telling his managers that he was re-assigning work from them to their direct reports.

My question to him was, "How are you developing your people if you re-assign work when you don't get an immediate response when you want it?" Of course he knew the answer because he was book smart. It was at that point that we had the opportunity to talk about the lack of alignment of his intentions with his words and actions and how his frustration would continue. He would get more of the same behavior from his managers until he clearly stated expectations, provided tools, resources and time frames and started holding his managers accountable if the results and time frames weren't met.

He also had to learn to provide reasonable time lines for completion and then wait for them to produce results.

Being a "smart rat," this client said it wasn't whether he knew what to do but whether he felt like doing the right thing in developing his people. The key would be in giving up control, having patience, being available to coach or guide and learning to trust others to get the job done, even if they did it differently from how he would have done it.

This is a good example of coaching a Type A leader, who might look and sound like a Type T leader on the surface. He was more concerned about his own results, controlling others and satisfying his needs first, while pretending to grow and develop others. It's just part of the process that a transformational leader understands, can distinguish and knows how to focus back on the alignment of intentions, actions and results. But if you're listening through your own filter, you'll miss the opportunity. Not surprisingly, this client concluded the coaching process at the end of the contract. Basically, he knew that his approach was not going to produce the results he wanted but didn't want to change how he managed.

Listening for Alignment

As you listen for alignment, you're first focused on the content of the message. As you begin to master listening at a higher level with others for alignment of thoughts, words and actions, then you can begin to listen to the emotions behind the message and pay attention to the vibrational energy of the conversation.

This process is what will begin to distinguish you as a masterful transformational, authentic leader. When you are listening deeply to the other person's message, your point of view ceases to exist. None of your own filters are present. At first, this is a very weird experience. I remember the first several times when I experienced this as a relatively new coach. While I had had years of training in communication and listening skills and transformational leadership practices, the experience of being totally outside myself as I listened to my clients was a bit unnerving.

The pattern that emerged was that I would cease taking notes during the process and, at the end, I had little recollection of what had been discussed. At first, I thought I had totally lost it. Then, at the end of the coaching sessions, I would ask my clients to recap what they had gained from the session and how they planned to take action. It was then that I realized I was so far into their listening, so to speak, that I was able to coach and guide totally based on what they needed, not what I wanted to tell them.

At first I didn't trust myself or the process. But as my clients would return and report the successes they experienced, I began to trust my intuition and trust my capacity to let go of controlling the process. Even to this day, though, as a transformational listener, it's important to do the self-checks to be sure you're not placing your own judgments or advice based on what has worked for you in the past. One way to do a self-check when providing advice based on your own experience is to specifically state that it's your experience and ask them if they think the example or information could benefit them. You both need to take ownership of the process and know when your filter may add value or when your experience may interfere.

At this point, when you are listening for alignment and for their vibrational energy, you will intuitively know when something is "off." The words might be right, but your gut or intuition will tell you something's not right.

Many of us have had those feelings but discount them. The Type T leader will practice listening to the intuitive nudges and learn from them. This kind of listening takes more time. While bottom-line thinkers don't want to waste time, deep listening can save time and energy and money in the long run because there can be greater clarity, commitment and alignment with goals.

Digging Deep—Intuition

Remember Martin, the financial planner from Chapter 2? It's time to add the details and revisit his story, to get a better sense of what it "feels like" when we listen deeply and trust our intuition. He was one of my very first coaching clients, and I wasn't at the point of trusting my intuition. I remember brainstorming with him about "what he would do if he knew he wouldn't fail." We had an exhaustive list. And, at one point, he hesitated, reflected and then said, "No, that's not it . . . I do not want to do that," but didn't tell me what it was when I asked. My gut instinct was to probe the statement because his vibrational energy had changed. But I didn't. Two days later, he called and told me he knew what he was destined to be, as he claimed his higher purpose and was true to his authentic self. He said he felt called to leave his financial planning practice and become a minister. As you may remember, he later became a hospital chaplain. At the time of the initial discussion, he didn't want to acknowledge his true feelings, and, as a new coach, I wasn't confident in going beyond his resistance or exploring the unknown. As I have gained more confidence in my coaching and deep listening skills, I trust my intuition if I detect a lack of alignment in the other person's speaking or demeanor. I will explain that "something seems off" and inquire about it.

Reading the emotions behind the thoughts or the vibrational energy is a tricky matter and one not to take lightly. There is great responsibility that comes with this practice because peoples' lives and futures are at stake. The transformational leader knows this and honors this practice. The Type T leader has to be able to distinguish the authenticity and rawness of the heartfelt emotions of people who are earnestly yearning for personal freedom from the people who have the checklist, transaction mentality and those "acting-as-if" they are heartfelt and earnest.

Transactional vs. Transformational

As you embark on deliberately practicing this new communication style, know that it takes time to feel confident in your intuitive, deeper listening to others. It takes time for it to come naturally. My client, Natalie, who was itching to be promoted and had a goal of being a vice president *someplace* before she turned 40, was told that she needed to be softer, not so hard-lined. She was the classic Type A leader. Natalie was all business, all the time. She didn't have time for idle chitchat; there was work to do and people better get to work and produce results—so she could look good, although she would never have said that.

She was a diva. On casual Fridays, she dressed down by wearing a skirt, rather than a suit and casual heels, rather than professional looking pumps. Rather than the colors or logo apparel of the local NFL team and jeans, she wore tailored pants and a jacket. Wearing team sports clothing was pure silliness and considered unprofessional for Natalie.

Her communication with her team was terse and to the point. It was directive and bitchy. While she thought she was being clear and stating expectations, it came across as demanding and controlling. She viewed her peers as subordinates because she had been in her position longer, and she thought she had nothing to learn or gain by associating with them. So when she was told that she distanced herself from the team, that didn't really bother her nor did she understand the importance or value of teamwork with peers and direct reports.

Imagine her dismay when she learned that she would never be promoted unless she learned how to play nice with her colleagues and be nice to her staff. There was no room for "nice" on her corporate ladder to success.

So, when it came time to participate in management coaching, she actually relished the idea because she could check it off her list and move on to seeking the next promotion. Her preparation was perfunctory. Her self-reflections and learning from the required reading lists were basically book reports. In her mind, she was doing what was expected. It was a checklist to the path of promotion.

Natalie was a tough nut to crack. And yet, I knew how she yearned to succeed. I could see myself in her on many levels when I was her age. And how do you train someone that it's about transformation not transaction? Bottom line is that you can't. All you can do is *coach* and *advise*, which is what I did with Natalie. We talked about not only the importance of teamwork with colleagues and peers but ways that she could demonstrate it. What it looked like. What it sounded like, so she could mimic or copy it. Some things were funny regarding how she wanted to approach getting to know her colleagues on a more personal level to work with them better. At first, she said she would "put a luncheon appointment on their calendar" telling them the date, time and place and purpose of the meeting—i.e. to get to know each other better. I suggested that might be more of the same directive and controlling behavior that distanced her from and annoyed others. She then swung to the opposite end of the spectrum by wanting to schedule pedicures during the lunch hour. Again, we had to discuss that, while it was more personal and "girly," not everyone would be open to having a pedicure with someone they barely knew or even liked.

So we started with basics like sharing a little more herself and having a picture or two of her family on her desk and asking about their families or how their weekend was. We talked about the importance of her aligning her vibrational energy, while engaging in conversation and really listening with interest. After two weeks, she reported that she had mastered that and people were really responding well. Everything had turned around for the better, and she was grateful to have learned this skill.

She was delusional about how she thought that two weeks could turn relationships around. She was unrealistic and only saw what she wanted to see. Natalie and I had a conversation about how people may not trust this new behavior after two weeks. When people are accustomed to cold and calculating behavior and responses, most likely, they will be skeptical of such a dramatic shift. After two months of practiced and learned behavior, Natalie applied for the next level management position. To her dismay, her bosses praised her for turning the trend, but they needed to know that it was sustainable for longer periods of time and, especially, when the inevitable challenges occurred. Most people revert to old behaviors when under stress or pressure. So, unless new behaviors have been practiced and in place for longer periods of time, most people are unable to sustain some positive communication in stressful situations.

Natalie's desire for bigger titles, more money, more power and more perks was overwhelming. If she couldn't get that promotion with her current employer, she'd find it someplace else, which she did. While people wished her well in her new position, there was a collective sigh of relief that they didn't have to deal with her obsessive, controlling and demeaning style.

In developing your collaborative communication style, trust is essential and multifaceted. Not only do you have to learn to trust yourself, but you have to learn to trust others. You need to learn to trust the process of collaborative communication. Collaboration is about doing what's for the good of the whole, trusting that it will work out for the good of all and listening to the intuitive nudges, learning from them.

Creating
a Type T Culture

Chapter 12

Developing a Vision

In previous chapters, when I talked about creating a personal vision and your own key words, I touched on how these concepts have also been applied in organizational settings. Now we're going to incorporate all you've learned and start applying the concepts to an external focus, external processes and the intended outcomes that will be for the good of the whole for whatever group you choose to lead.

Reminder: For the sake of simplicity, the term "organization" refers to for-profit companies, not-for-profit organizations, associations, religious or spiritual groups and volunteer groups. The organization can be any size, from two people to thousands.

Organizational Culture

I once heard someone trying to describe the meaning of organizational culture to another and after several attempts said, "Well, it's like trying to nail Jell-O to a tree." Aside from a funny image, it's pretty true. Organizational culture is something you feel or sense. It's not any one thing that says "this is our culture," but an accumulation of small details, patterns of behavior and often the unspoken codes of conduct. It's been described as "the way we do things around here." And just like families, there are accepted ways of doing things, traditions, skeletons in the closet, the "accepted" look and spoken language that identify the clan that says either you fit in or you're the black sheep. The same holds true in organizations.

And as I said, even families have their own culture and dynamic, which becomes very evident when families are blended due to marriage and divorce. The same applies here.

From an organizational standpoint, the culture represents a collective body of thoughts, words, actions and vibrational energy all its own. Effective and successful organizational leaders are intentional about creating the culture and vibe of their organization. Unfortunately, the majority of organizations take a piecemeal approach, try to apply cookie-cutter concepts and end up with a one-size fits all, mish-mash mess.

It starts with two main components: the vision and the core values or "key words" of the organization introduced earlier. Just as you embarked on creating your own vision and key words for your authentic self and purpose, an organization must do the same.

How the Kansas City Ballet Created a New Vision

The vision becomes the guidepost from which all else emanates—including culture. It is big and bold. It inspires and excites people, who want to be part of something that is bigger than themselves.

Several years ago, I had the opportunity to facilitate a strategic planning session for the Kansas City Ballet Board of Directors. With permission from the board president at the time, I am able to tell their story of redefining their culture, as a wonderful illustration of the power and impact of creating a contemporary and compelling culture.

It was 2007 and excavation had started for a new, world-class performing arts center in Kansas City, which would be the new home for the ballet when the center opened in 2011. The organization was also in the middle of a large capital campaign to renovate a historic building that would house the ballet school and administrative offices.

The purpose of the planning meeting was to not only address some key organizational and operational issues, but to set a strategic direction that would be aligned with the impending new locations for both the school and performances at the new performing arts center.

"We're Not New York!"

One board member described the ballet as a "good ballet company" but not world class. Others said they were a good regional ballet company in a "flyover state." (Translation: one of those states you fly over from New York to California.)

The conversation shifted to: "How can we transform from good to world-class before taking the stage of a world class performing arts center on opening night in 2011?"

The first response was, "WE'RE NOT NEW YORK!"

No one has ever really confused Kansas City with New York, but the question then became, "What can we be, if we're not New York?"

They had to envision a whole new future because the new performing arts center was already gaining international acknowledgement for design and innovation. The board knew they had to go beyond the past perceptions of being a good ballet company and a good school and live into the acclaim of performing in a world-class structure.

After some gut-wrenching discussions, someone quietly said, "We could be a dance destination point."

You could have heard a pin drop at that point. What did it mean to be a "dance destination point?"

All of a sudden, the room became electrified! The energy shifted from being a victim to the glory of New York legends to becoming a powerful destination point in the world of dance. They envisioned events like world premieres, a place for training for artistic directors and a museum and archive for ballet. The list of ideas flowed effortlessly and with excitement.

The vision was big and it was bold and it was the start of creating a whole new culture for the organization.

Essential Elements to Creating a New Vision

There are some essential elements that occurred in this example that are worth noting. As I describe these, think about how the concepts can be applied in your organization.

Clarity

A first step is to start with a clear picture of the current environment, perceptions and realities. For the ballet, the reality was that they were good but not world class.

Next, it's important to be very clear about what you want to be and where you want to go with your vision for the future. The clearer the description of the future vision, the better.

- How will you know when you reached that vision?
- What will it look like?
- What will people be saying about it?
- What will it feel like to be in that environment?
- What results will be produced?

Catalyst

When you have a big and bold vision, it will be a catalyst for all other actions. The new vision becomes a catalyst for newfound energy that was lacking before. It becomes a catalyst for commitment.

Facilitation

When you have a clear picture of your future vision, it will facilitate all other goals and action plans. It will become the backdrop for organizational decisions and choices. It will also be the checkpoint to ensure alignment.

Alignment

A clear vision facilitates the alignment of people, resources, expenditures, structure, policies and practices. Just as you've gone through the process of aligning your own thoughts, words and actions with your future vision, organizations need to do the same to create a high performance and healthy culture.

For example, the ballet had to change its language to reflect this new vision of being a world-class ballet company and a dance destination point. Internally, as well as externally, the ballet was being referred to as a destination for dance. The school was no longer called the ballet school. When they opened the new building that housed the administrative offices and "school," it was called The Center for Dance and Creativity. Do you see the power of aligning the words with the future vision now? It's more compelling and exciting, and it opens the doors to so many more possibilities.

It Takes Courage to Create a New Vision

It's important to note, at this point, that as you embark on a new vision, not everyone will be aligned with it. There will be resisters and naysayers. And the same was true for some of the board members. It takes courage to set a new course. There is no room for people who want to blame or make excuses or deny the need for change. It takes courage to have the right people in the right seats on the bus that is moving in a new direction—one that will ultimately change the organization's culture.

And, like many organizations going through significant changes like this, there were some board members who were not aligned and chose to step down. They were thanked for their participation, support and contributions for helping the ballet achieve the success to date. Then there was room for new board members who would be aligned with the new direction.

When the wheels start turning, all of the decision makers and implementers need to take ownership and accountability for contributing to the forward direction. It takes courage. It takes being consistent and persistent in pursuit of that vision.

For the Kansas City Ballet, their courage paid off. Three and a half years after creating the vision, and a year before they would take the stage at the new performing arts center, *The Kansas City Star* newspaper made a bold statement about the new and improved Kansas City Ballet: "Kansas City will be for dance, what Sundance is for film."

Wow. This statement reflects the impact and power of creating a bold vision. It infers that because of the direction of the ballet company, the city will be known for dance, and all of the dance community will be part of it. It wasn't about just the ballet anymore. It was about all of the city and all forms of dance. The vision was expansive and inclusionary.

On a side note, there were other acknowledgements that contributed to the success of creating and confirming the new vision. Over the years, many board members made regular trips to New York City to attend ballet performances. They had established connections and relationships with the ballet community there. In 2012, members of Mikhail Barishnokoff's studio planned a trip to Kansas City to learn more about the Center for Dance and Creativity and the innovations of this dance community.

So, while the ballet board in Kansas City had said, "We're not New York!" the New York dance community had taken note and was saying, "We need to go to see what Kansas City is doing!"

Chapter 13

Creating Core Values

When it comes to your vision transformation, think big, dream big. People want to be part of something bigger than themselves. I can't emphasize enough how important this is. As we drill down through the next section of the book about how to create and instill a higher level of leadership at the organizational level, the vision will be your guide.

When it comes to your "mission," think of it as your reason for existing. Why does your company, your division, your department exist? What is its purpose? What are you there to fulfill and for whom? Typically, a mission statement is just a couple of sentences long. The reader will know what you do, why you do it and what distinguishes you from all others.

But a mission statement, regardless of how well it's done, is still a statement—a very important one. So, what is behind the implementation of the vision? I will tell you it's my next favorite component to clarifying a vision —core values. This wasn't always the case.

I remember when the concept of core values was introduced many years ago, and I was very cynical about the idea. To me, it seemed like just another version of "Flavor of the Month" management whims.

Remember that organizational leaders are often looking for the next big thing to make people better leaders, better communicators, more effective delegators or managers. No sooner had companies invested tens of thousands of dollars in training and fancy rollouts for implementation and making sure everyone was on board, than the next shiny object came along and the old "best new thing" was declared ineffective. It was on to the next program.

When the concept of core values came along, companies jumped on the bandwagon. More relevant companies had focus groups of employees to determine their values, but many corporate core values were handed down from on high. Posters were plastered around buildings, employee badges were remade to remind people about the values, and they were told to wear them proudly. Yet, if you asked employees what the values were, they usually had to turn the badge over to read them to you. Many companies would have Core Value of the Month. This month we're focused on "Integrity!" Next month, "Service!" To me, it seemed like the hoopla around the monthly initiative reinforced the idea that when the month was over, we could go back to our old ways and pretend to practice the current month's value.

Usually there was a lot of eye-rolling by employees with these initiatives, and many just kept their heads down waiting for them to pass by—resignedly awaiting the next big thing.

Here are some classic examples of core values that illustrate the lack of alignment with operating practices and policies.

Can you guess the company that had these core values?

- Communication.
- Excellence.
- Respect.
- Integrity.

Hint: In just 15 years, it grew from nowhere to become America's seventh largest company, employing 21,000 employees in more than 40 countries. *Fortune* magazine named this company "America's Most Innovative Company" for six consecutive years from 1996 to 2001.

Enron.

Some people reading this may not even remember Enron now. But this company was the darling of Wall Street until everything blew up. The movie *The Smartest Guys In The Room* was an excellent documentary of the rise and fall of the company and its corporate leaders. There was no integrity in their business. There was no respect for the customers, the employees or their shareholders.

Interestingly, Ken Lay, the son of a preacher who created the company and fell from grace, was indicted by a grand jury on 11 counts of securities fraud and could have faced 25 - 30 years in prison. But three and a half months before his sentencing, he died of a heart attack. It makes me wonder about the impact of emotion on our bodies. As we talked about earlier, the research from the Institute for Advanced Theoretical Research found that the emotion of *shame* has the worst impact on a person's physical body, if experienced for long periods of time. I've often wondered if Ken Lay died from shame.

Let's look at another example of crazy misaligned core values. These are the core values of General Motors:

- Customer enthusiasm.
- Integrity.
- Teamwork.
- Innovation.
- Continuous improvement.
- Individual respect and responsibility.

What kind of corporate culture would choose not to make a repair that would cost 57 cents per vehicle that resulted in more than two dozen deaths and a cover-up that lasted nine years with more than 2.6 million cars recalled?

Prior to this shocking disclosure and recall, in 2009, approximately $1.5 billion was used in TARP funds, as part of the government bailout to keep GM and its major suppliers afloat. Countless makes and models of automobiles were eliminated during this time because they were bleeding dollars from the bottom line. More than 30 makes and models were discontinued when the government bailout occurred.

It makes me wonder what the leadership team and the board of directors were thinking when they continued making cars that were not only defective, but massively unprofitable. I find it interesting that so many large companies that espouse decisions to be based on improving the bottom line can be so blind to the obvious. There was no integrity in their decision making or in honoring their fiduciary responsibilities to the shareholders, when they continued making cars they knew had defective ignitions and brakes in some models and other models that lost massive amounts of money year after year.

The point is that core values are nothing, if the business practices are not aligned. They become a farce and a demotivator to employees who really know the difference.

Core Values That Mean Something

Some of the more contemporary and successful companies have core values that reflect their vision in ways that are fun and inspiring. Google is a good example:

- We want to work with great people.
- Technology innovation is our lifeblood.
- Working here is fun.
- Be actively involved.
- Don't take success for granted.
- Do the right thing, and don't be evil.
- Earn customer and user loyalty and respect every day.
- Sustainable long term growth and profitability are keys to our success.
- We care about and support the communities where we work and live.
- We aspire to improve and change the world.

Take a close look at the combination of these statements. These values are very clear about their purpose and how they want to operate both internally and externally. "We aspire to change the world." This is the kind of statement to which most people would say, "I want to contribute to that! I want to work for a company that is fun and wants to do the right thing." This is the expectation of the people who work there.

Zappos is another great example:

- Embrace and drive change.
- Create fun and a little weirdness.
- Be adventurous, creative and open-minded.
- Pursue growth and learning.
- Build a positive team and family spirit.
- Be passionate and determined.
- Be humble.

What I love about Zappos is that the interview process includes questions about how candidates have demonstrated these core values in past jobs and how they can contribute to the company in the future. I had heard that if the hiring manager had difficulty deciding between candidates, "be humble" was the one that was the determining factor.

Think about how your company would be different if the core value "be humble" was a determining factor in hiring new employees.

I prefer to use the term "key words" when working on a personal vision, as you read earlier, or when creating a new vision or culture for a department or organization. Key words (aka core values) help direct an organizational vision just as they do a personal one.

These key words will describe what you want your department or company to be known for. The words become the "backdrop" for how people are hired, operating policies and practices, decisions regarding products and services and how people interact.

Just as we created the key words for your personal leadership vision, the process is much the same for a department or organization. Only this time, ideally, you will involve as many people as possible in the process.

Four Steps to Creating Organizational Key Words

Here are four steps to help you get started:

Step One: Brainstorm and create a list of words that the team or company "culture committee" would like the department or organization to be known for. List as many words as you can and get input from every one.

Step Two: Have each person vote on their top three words, assigning three points for the word they like best, two points for second choice and one point for their third choice.

Step Three: For each word on the list, tally the number of points, based on how many people chose it as number one, two or three. For example, if four people chose "integrity" as #1 =12 points, 5 as #2 = 10 points and 1 as #3 = 1 point. Total points for integrity = 23 points

Step Four: Take a look at your top five or six words that the group voted on and discuss how these words would add value to the culture you're trying to create or the vision you have for the future. There usually is a robust discussion about each word and how it's distinguished from other words. And I've seen it happen when a word doesn't make "the cut" to the final five words but through discussion gets back on the list!

For example, I worked with employees for a public works department, who wanted to change their image and perception among the municipal employees and community. In the past, they said they'd been considered the "black sheep" and police, fire and first responders got all the glory. They said no one paid attention to them unless streets weren't plowed in winter or traffic lights weren't working. The team had a reputation for being negative, whiney and distrustful of management and each other. They weren't happy and were tired of this image.

We embarked on the process of defining their key words. The foremen decided they wanted their teams to be part of the process too, so they took all of the words back to their teams, conducted the voting process and brought their top words back to the group. New words had been added, and many were dropped off the list. Discussion and voting ensued. One foreman was passionate about a word that was a late addition: "pioneering." When he explained why his team liked the word and how it could help the team in creating the future they yearned for, everyone agreed that it would be one of the top five words. Their top five words are now:

United Accountable Dedicated Trustworthy Pioneering

I think these were terrific words for the future they wanted to create, but more importantly, they were proud of how the teams worked together and collaborated and are excited about putting the words into action! They have ownership of the process and the results and the implementation. This is a great example of aligning thoughts, words and actions as they created their new vision.

Know that some team members may not buy into the process or the results. And that's part of the process, too—for the team to work with resisters or, eventually, to move on without them. When the positive momentum starts with a future vision, there's excitement and hope, and people like that positive feeling.

Recruitment and Selection Based on Core Values

When I first started working with a rural hospital to create a culture of accountability, their patient satisfaction scores were in the bottom 5% on a national scale. Surveys related to employee morale showed satisfaction levels were well below 50% for most of the categories. We embarked on creating a "culture committee" that had people from throughout the hospital and at varying levels in the organization. There were people who were in management and non-management, hourly and salaried people and the demographics of the group were representative of the general population at the hospital. The key criteria was that they had to want to be part of creating a healthier, happier and more productive workplace. In other words, they had to care about the future of the hospital.

It's important to remember that this hospital was so far removed from other professional organizations that the employees, managers included, were "professionally isolated." The prison was the only larger employer in the county of 4500. The town had fewer than 2000 people and the nearest Wal-Mart was 100 miles away. Most people had grown up in the ranching community and had little exposure to other organizational best practices—and they did just fine, thank you very much. Or so they thought.

But the world of patient care was changing dramatically. People had greater choices regarding where to receive care based on new technologies, while government funding for community hospitals was shrinking and was based on meeting patient satisfaction scores and overall efficiencies. They simply could not continue to operate the way they always had, even though things in the town remained relatively the same as they had been 30 or 40 years ago. Recruiting and retaining qualified medical staff was almost impossible because there was no local talent with advanced skills and education, and no one wanted to move there. It was equally hard to find and retain non-medical professionals, such as IT, HR and accounting professionals. Basically, the administrative or maintenance positions and non-exempt positions were the only ones that could be filled with local people, and the skill level was relatively low. And attitudes were worse.

We had our work cut out for us, starting with creating the awareness that the hospital would not survive if patient satisfaction, employee performance and quality standards did not improve. We started by creating a list of "key words" that would be used as core values. Given that 99% of the people were unfamiliar with core values, why they were important and how they could be used, there was a lot of behind-the-scenes education, which some of the culture committee embraced enthusiastically, and some did not. I assured the enthusiastic members of the team that we had to be consistent and persistent in our pursuit to model the key words, which became their "7 Keys to the Culture" and that the people who did not want to work in a positive healthy culture would eventually "deselect" themselves and leave. And they would say, "But there's no place for them to go…" Crossing my fingers and hoping that my past experiences wouldn't let me down, I assured them it would happen, even if there were no place else for them to work in the community. At about the six-month mark of our work together, the most promising manager excitedly told me that it was starting to happen! The negative, toxic people were leaving the hospital. When I asked where they were going, all she could say was, "I don't know! But all the negative people are leaving!"

At the same time, the CEO had started interviewing the final candidates for each position to be filled. He reviewed the Get Out of B.E.D. model and the 7 Keys to the Culture with them. He explained the desired future culture of the hospital and why it was important, not only for the employees and patients, but also for the community as a whole. He would then ask them questions about how they had demonstrated each of the Keys in previous positions and how they could contribute to the culture of the hospital in the future.

After 18 months of concentrated training, coaching and reinforcement with the management team, the culture committee and many employees throughout the hospital, the patient satisfaction scores increased dramatically, and the employee morale survey scores increased 15.1% over the previous year and were 22.4% higher than the national average.

During the time we worked together, the hospital also lost a third of its funding through government cutbacks. This could have devastated the hospital, not only financially, but in terms of morale and quality of care, but the team was stronger and more adept at handling adversity and having healthier communication.

Interestingly, one department that received the lowest rankings for quality and morale was the housekeeping department. Some significant changes were made in staffing and the CEO's interview process was a key component in changing who was hired. The net effect was that patient satisfaction scores started to climb after more attention was paid to the hiring of the housekeeping staff. At first glance, it may not seem like a direct connection, but the housekeeping staff had the most frequent and most consistent contact with the patients than anyone else in the hospital. More than the doctors and more than the nurses. The housekeeping staff brought patients their meals, removed trays and cleaned the patient rooms several times a day. The more friendly and caring the housekeeping staff was, the happier the patients were with their overall experience at the hospital.

This is a great example of the importance of every position and how each position contributes to the greater whole. It is not unlike Disney's practice of providing extensive customer service training to cleanup crews at the parks because guests are more likely to ask a street sweeper for information than to go to the information booth.

Another way that the hospital and many organizations keep core values alive and an integral part of the culture is to incorporate them into performance review discussions, as a way to reinforce desired behavior. A housekeeping person at another rural hospital described one of the key responsibilities of her position as "preventing infection." This is a great example of a person understanding the bigger picture and importance of her position. She took great pride in her role because of that.

New employee orientations are also often revamped to include a discussion about culture, its importance and how each person has a role in making the organization great. It's about creating an environment where employees feel accountable and included in the future. They can be part of creating something bigger than themselves and take pride in their individual and collective contributions.

Clearly, creating unique key words or core values for a department or organization can have a big impact. When designed and implemented with clear intentions and involvement, there is a positive impact on individual performance, morale, employee engagement and ultimately, organizational results.

Chapter 14

Components of a Positive Culture

How Human Resource Functions Demonstrate and Reinforce Corporate Culture

Remember, corporate culture is loosely defined as "how we do things around here." In many organizations, job candidates and employees look to the human resources department and the leadership teams to put the structures in place for them to be successful in their jobs. People get a feel for a company's culture long before they accept a position, starting with the recruitment, selection and onboarding processes.

Here are some high-level examples of how you can start implementing human resource practices in your organization that will start shifting the trend to a healthier culture.

Recruitment, Selection and Onboarding

Make sure your job descriptions are up-to-date and reflect the current role, impact and accountabilities of the position. Job descriptions have multiple uses and are a pivotal tool in effective management and alignment of people, functions and results, as well as corporate compliance.

Your job descriptions will be your primary source for screening qualified candidates. During the recruitment and selection process, not only do you need to be asking questions about a candidate's capacity to perform the duties of the job, but you need to be asking questions to be sure the candidate selected is a good cultural fit to the organization. Just as Zappos interviews candidates based on their core values, more and more organizations are doing this as well.

Forbes and *U.S. News and World Reports* highlighted some developing workplace trends that are sobering at best. For example, only 40% of employees are still engaged after their first six months on the job and 70 - 84% of employees are currently job hunting. So what are you doing to engage new employees and retain them?

Do you have an onboarding process that will connect people to the organization, it's vision, the people and how they can contribute to the future? Many times, new employees are shown where they sit and where the bathrooms are and then left to fend for themselves. For some, onboarding means filling out reams of paperwork and listening to someone drone on about insurance plans. By creating a buddy system, people can learn the ropes, meet colleagues and help them get acclimated to their new environment. Regardless of the position, people want to feel valued when they start a new job. They want to know they made the right decision to join your organization and can be successful. Type T leaders know this is important at an organizational and department/unit level and make sure the right processes are in place to welcome new people in a way that makes them want to stay and be part of the future.

Compensation and Culture

Other key components to creating a healthy culture that will impact employee retention are the compensation structure and practices. An organization's compensation philosophy needs to reflect the corporate values, and the right systems need to be in place to assure there is integrity in the process. Again, starting with job descriptions, positions need to be benchmarked internally and externally, to assure competitive rates of pay and that accurate pay ranges are established. Then, the administration of equitable compensation practices must be adhered to, not only by HR but by operational and sales management teams as well. For example, it's not uncommon for sales teams to establish specific goals at the beginning of the year for the sales staff. Whether it's by-product line, geography, volume, cross-sells or up-sells, to change a compensation system or sales goals in the middle of the year is a total disincentive to people who are, in many cases, paid on a commission-only basis. The end result is a great distrust of management when they mess with people's pay and income potential midway through the year. It's amazing how many of the companies that do this also espouse that their employees are their greatest asset.

Another compensation faux pas has to do with "compression." Compression occurs when salary ranges are adjusted to accommodate market conditions and new hires start at a rate of pay that is either very close to or the same as someone who has been in the job for a couple years and received market rate merit increases. Oftentimes, managers will gerrymander the system and create "promotions" to give a bigger raise to existing employees, when, in fact, job duties haven't changed at all. Or worse, employees game the system by getting another job at a different company at a higher rate of pay. Then their existing company counteroffers at the new rate or higher to keep a valued employee.

Either way, gerrymandering the compensation system to get equitable rates of pay for high-performing people is not a good practice or a demonstration of valuing employees. There's no integrity in the system. It's best to have human resources policies and practices that are fair and equitable, so people don't have to game the system. Unfortunately, many HR professionals are so driven by "administrivia" and threatened by guidelines rather than rules, that it can be difficult for more enlightened leaders to work within a system like that. The Type T leaders will need to work collaboratively within the system to raise the bar on some of the operational and HR policies and practices like the ones mentioned.

Employee Benefits and Culture

Another area that requires alignment and reflects organizational culture and demographics is employee benefits. Benefit packages for companies that have a healthy corporate culture and have Type

T leadership are going to be progressive, contemporary and relevant to the employee demographics. The benefit needs of the Baby Boomers are very different from those of the Gen X and even more different from the desires of the Gen Y employees.

Traditional pension plans are a thing of the past and flexible benefit packages will be the best way to attract and retain the employees who will be the best fit and most productive in your corporate culture. Benefits must reflect not only the core values of an organization, but the values of the people you want to attract. The benefits offered at Google or Zappos or Twitter will attract the people who will be contributors in those kinds of high-tech environments. Law firms, engineering firms and accounting practices, which tend to have an older, perhaps more traditional, workforce will have a whole different array of benefits that will appeal to the demographics for their high-performing employees.

Employee Development and Culture

Training and employee development is another area that has a significant impact on the culture of an organization and retention of talented people. Healthy cultures encourage continuous learning, and it doesn't always require a formalized program to instill this mindset. It could be starting a group and holding robust discussion about the content of a leadership book, evaluating and applying the content to their organization, while keeping realistic expectations. The rural hospital I worked with that is referenced in a previous chapter, is a good example of this. The staff of the hospital was "professionally isolated." Most of the management team acknowledged that they did not read books about management or leadership. The CEO started a reading program with the management team with one book, *Good to Great,* by Jim Collins. I had referenced it many times when working with them and despite the moans and groans of having to read a book, they did and they ended up having some powerful discussions about leadership practices.

I've also seen managers who go to the other extreme in professional development, when there is not a professional development program in place. Some overachieving Type A managers have their teams reading two to four books a month and require them to discuss the books at manager's meetings. While this is all well and good, it can create a bit of leadership schizophrenia, lots of theory and little implementation.

The bottom line is that continuing professional development is a key factor in creating a healthy corporate culture and must reflect the values of the company. In the absence of a formalized program, the Type T leader knows how to construct an independent approach to achieve the same result, which is to coach and mentor employees to a higher level of performance and leadership.

Job Design and Structure

Another way to instill and reinforce a healthy culture has to do with job design, job structure and work environment. Companies with healthy organizational cultures are paying attention to job design and the content of the job, so that it is not only meeting the needs of the organization to serve clients or customers, but is designed in a way that can be fulfilling to the person performing the job or at least a stepping stone to more fulfilling work. Job structures and design must first and foremost meet the organizational vision, mission and objectives to serve its constituencies. But job design has changed dramatically in the past 5 - 10 years due to technology, demographics and competing in a global society. Many organizations have positions that are nontraditional, where there are virtual work environments and more telecommuting, independent contractors and job sharing than ever before.

The changing demographics of the workplace are demanding new job structures to meet customer and employee expectations. The transformational leader understands that, in order to fulfill a higher purpose of leadership, new structures, policies and practices are required.

Stories, Rites and Rituals Create Culture

Corporate Cultures: the Rites and Rituals of Corporate Life by Terrence Deal and Allan Kennedy was my bible when I was working with an entrepreneurial company in Green Bay, Wisconsin. We were a small company with 250 employees when I started, and when I left 11 years later, we were a billion dollar, national company with over 1,700 employees. In addition, the company had been bought and sold about three times while I was there. I religiously followed the foundations that Deal and Kennedy outlined in creating a healthy corporate culture, which I believe contributed to the success and capacity to grow the company during that time.

Every organization has its own culture, which can be shaped, molded and modified. But it can never be duplicated or borrowed from another organization. I remember people trying to duplicate some of the things we did at the company in Green Bay with minimal success—despite giving them the complete plan and rollout of different initiatives. But the plan and the rollouts were unique to our culture and reflected our environment. It's kind of like taking a family tradition and imposing it on another family. It just doesn't feel right or have the same impact.

There are some key components that I applied from Deal and Kennedy's book, not only at the company in Green Bay, but when I was the vice president of human resources at subsequent employers and now use as a consultant facilitating culture change with client organizations. I highly recommend it as a resource for more ideas on corporate culture.

Stories about your organization and the rites and rituals that are unique to your company are the foundations for creating the culture you want. What stories are you telling and repeating? How are stories used in new employee orientation? Do your stories connect people so they have a sense of the past and a direction for the future? Are the stories compelling and inclusive? Can new employees see themselves as part of the growth and future?

Stories must be carefully crafted and intentional to reflect what you want, not what you don't want. No one wants to hear the war stories, except the current employees when the stories reflect overcoming significant obstacles to achieve a great goal. The implementation of the new system, rollout of a new product line, expansion to multiple locations or overcoming adversity and achieving success are the things that can align people with the spirit and attitude that you want to perpetuate. People learn from the stories they hear. So what stories are you and your team telling? Are they made of the stuff that builds the character that you want?

Who are the heroes of the organization? Who are the heroes in the stories? And do your heroes represent the core values that you want perpetuated?

What are your rites of passage in your organization? What is celebrated? What accomplishments are recognized? Each of these, whether formal or informal, provides clues to the culture of what it takes to be successful. I remember a young woman lawyer who was praised for working late and bringing her toddler back to work to finish a project. Yet her male colleague was praised for taking time off for his son's soccer game, being a family man and balancing work and career. These kinds of acknowledgements and inconsistencies do not go unnoticed by the average employee. Rites of passage and formal and informal acknowledgements communicate what it takes to be successful or what it takes to fit in— i.e. "the way we do things around here." Type T leaders take the time to make sure the application of rewards is consistent with the culture they want and that there are no double standards or mixed messages. The message is consistent and aligned with the values of the organization.

Meetings and Culture

Meetings are a whole subset of culture that need close examination. But suffice it to say that you need to look at each and every one of your meetings to see if they reflect the culture that you want. Everything from starting and ending on time, to how the purpose and anticipated outcomes are communicated, to how people

communicate during and after the meeting. If more business decisions are made outside of the meetings, then that will give you an
indication of the effectiveness of the meeting. Meeting attendance,
participation and behavior reflect the culture better than any other
visible structure. If you want to shift the culture, start with your
meetings. The purpose, intended outcomes, invitees and agenda
need to be transparent. People are accountable for attending and
not sending a person in their place unless it is appropriate. There is
the expectation and agreement that people follow through on their
commitments and that there is integrity throughout the process.

Communication and Culture

Your internal and external communications also reflect the culture
of the organization. What does your website say about the culture
by its look and feel, its content and layout? Think about your sales
brochures, your employee guides and annual reports. How do you
communicate to your employees and customers? One client company, in an effort to communicate better with their employees,
went into overdrive by sending "packets" to the employees' homes,
so family members would be included in the information, such as
benefit plans or information about strategic initiatives. The packets were voluminous and expensive. Many employees admitted to
throwing them away upon receipt, or they were left on the counter
with junk mail.

Another company realized that forms given to new employees on
their first day had been photocopied so many times that they were
a mess. They weren't aligned on the page, the ink was faded, even
creases from folded pages were imprinted on the documents. What
does the sloppy image on the documents convey to a new employee?
It certainly didn't convey a culture of quality.

Keep in mind that as you create and enhance your culture to be
healthier, more productive and more profitable, any written or visual communication must reflect the demographics of the intended
audience. Just as employee benefits and training need to reflect the

demographics of current and future employees, the communication medium needs to meet the market it is intended to reach.

The thoughts, words and vibes of the various communication channels must also clearly reflect the culture you're trying to reinforce or create. It can be very subtle but extremely powerful. Intentional Type T leaders realize this and are careful in how they craft their messages, internally and externally. It's amazing how Type A leaders can have little regard for the power of alignment in their words and the culture they're creating. One CEO I worked for was a former Viet Nam marine pilot. He was all business all the time. The bottom line ruled. And he would start every year with his "annual austerity campaign" as a way to reduce costs. Most people rolled their eyes and went about their business in their usual ways. Except me. I told him that I really didn't jump out of bed every day thinking, "How can I be more austere today?" Yet, I couldn't resist the opportunity to suggest a more positive way to get alignment with what he wanted. Since he wanted greater profits, how about a "profit maximization campaign?" At this point, he rolled his eyes at me and went about his business, as usual.

Ironically, but not surprisingly, many years ago I saw a similar type of profit maximization program at my company in Green Bay that was very successful and had employees engaged and excited to be part of the process.

As you can see, creating a healthy and effective corporate culture is clearly not a one-pronged approach—not even two or three. It is and needs to be comprised of programs and processes that are holistic, aligned with the vision of the organization and consistent with core values.

Chapter 15

Dollars and "Sense" of Corporate Culture

Building a healthy organizational culture is more than a feel-good process. A healthy culture can impact the bottom line both directly and indirectly. In a healthy culture, there is transparency, effective communication and sound leadership practices. An enlightened leadership team not only understands the importance of a healthy culture, but they are committed to having operational and human resource policies and practices and other support structures in place and aligned with the work environment.

Before we take a look at the financial impact and returns of a healthy culture, let's see what happens in an organization that lacks transparency and has poor communication.

Cost of Poor Communication During Times of Change

According to a U.S. Bureau of Labor Statistics study, there were significant effects on employee productivity and behavior during times of change. The study found that, as a direct consequence of organizational change, which could have been a result of a merger or acquisition, downsizing, change in leadership or, and I love this one, "a series of bad decisions…" there was a big impact on productivity. The study revealed:

- **Productivity dropped 75%** from 4.8 hours/day *to 1.2 hours/day.*
- Social chat and **gossip increased** from 1.5 hours/day *to 3.2 hours/day.*
- **Retraining increased 25%** from 0 hours to 1.8 hours per person.

Now, these figures seem rather shocking to most people. But what's even more shocking is that the study was released in *1997*.

That was before Twitter, Facebook, texting and instant messaging. In the age of heads-down, online communication, a 2013 study revealed that 16 minutes of every hour is spent on social media sites. That translates to about two hours each workday potentially sharing corporate dirty laundry. What makes it even more daunting is that messages are no longer confined to the water cooler or the confines of the building but can go globally and viral.

Unfortunately, I have not found recent figures from the Bureau of Labor Statistics (BLS) to compare, but based on my experience over the last 17 years and changes in technology, my guess is that productivity slumps to an all-time low when a leadership team chooses not to communicate clearly, timely or consistently during times of change.

To help put the numbers into perspective about the bottom-dollar impact for a company not communicating during times of change, let's look at some examples of potential impact.

NOTE: You can use your own company data to see the impact, but for the sake of simplicity, we'll use the numbers from the 1997 study and the most current average hourly rate in the United States to calculate the financial impact on productivity.

According to data reported in November 2013 from BLS, the average hourly rate in the private sector was $24.17. Salary plus benefits, which typically is about 30% in addition to base pay, would be about $31.00 per hour.

So, if people work 1.2 hrs and are not working 6.8 hours due to lack of communication, it costs the company about $211.00 per day per person in lost productivity.

10 employees = $2,110/day

100 employees = $21,100/day

Basically, if we use the BLS research from 1997 regarding lost productivity and apply it to current hourly rates and a company has 100 employees, there is a loss of over $21,000 per day due to poor or incomplete communication about changes that impact employees.

An enlightened, transformational leader understands this and is willing to carefully craft and plan communication to minimize confusion, misunderstandings and rampant rumor-mill rumblings. In a healthy culture, there is a proactive attempt to build trust and gain commitment and engagement from employees during times of change through clear and effective communication.

Rework and Turnover

Two other considerations regarding the costs associated with an unhealthy culture are turnover and rework costs. When there is an unhealthy culture, there can be a fairly high turnover rate. Unfortunately, in a negative culture, most of the people who leave are the ones who have marketable skills, good attitudes and the potential to contribute to a healthy environment. Often, the people who stay have less marketable skill sets and are the whiners, complainers and lower producers perpetuating an unhealthy culture.

Many times, organizations overlook the cost of turnover. Here's a quick rule of thumb for calculating those costs:

Base Pay = $50,000 + 30% for benefits = $65,000 for salary and benefits

Assume that it takes a person six months to become somewhat competent in the job and one year to be fully competent. If a person leaves after one year, your organization has spent $65,000 without having a fully competent person performing the function for a full 12 months.

Another person is hired, and the clock starts over. Assuming this person works out and stays for more than a year, the position now costs:

$130,000

+ recruiting expenses x 2

+ lost opportunity costs x 2

+ Hourly rate of the people who trained two people

+ Temporary costs or overtime of coworkers covering for open non-exempt positions

What might seem like a $50,000 year job has now become up to $200,000 after two years because of an unhealthy culture, poor hiring decisions and/or poor performance management.

Rework is a whole area that gets very little consideration, except in manufacturing facilities where costs per unit can more easily be determined. But, consider knowledge or information-based positions. The time spent in emails going back and forth for clarification, mistakes made due to not following directions, not reading an email completely, incomplete follow through and poor quality that results in rework is staggering. It's not uncommon to have six to ten email exchanges to clear up misunderstandings. Each email takes time and costs money because of the lack of attention to detail. In the information age where data is readily accessible, it's easy to say, "I'll resend it," which takes time away from completing original work.

So, after all that depressing news, let's look at the positive impact on the bottom line when there is a healthy culture and companies are socially responsible. Rajendra Sisodia, David Wolfe and Jag Sheth, authors of *Firms of Endearment: How World-Class Companies Profit from Passion and Purpose* share the results of a study in which they looked at companies that were especially socially responsible. They call these firms "Firms of Endearment" or FoEs. They compared the shareholder returns of these socially responsible firms with the S&P 500 and companies cited in *Good to Great* by Jim Collins. What they found was that the firms that were socially responsible outperformed the S&P 500 by 9x.

CORPORATE CULTURE FOCUS - ROI			
Investor Returns # Years	S&P	Good to Great	Firms of Endearment
3	38%	75%	73%
5	13%	77%	128%
10	122%	331%	1026%

In a healthy culture, not only will employees and shareholders feel good about the organization, but it can be good for the bottom line too! Type T leaders understand this and use their power positively to put the right structures, policies and practices in place to impact the bottom line.

Chapter 16

Creating Alignment and Commitment

One of the challenges of any leader is working with intact teams or teams that have been together longer than you have been their leader. They have their own culture, their own way of doing things and their own patterns of communication. Perhaps the biggest mistake a leader can make is to go into a position like the new sheriff in town, enforcing new rules and ways of doing things.

I learned this lesson the hard way many years ago, when I was promoted to vice president of human resources in a very traditional company. Despite the fact that I was hired to bring about change and help lead the workforce into the future, they really didn't want to change. There was one person in the human resource department who had started working there before I was born, and there was extensive documentation about policies and practices in the 1950's that could be referenced on a moment's notice.

At that point in my career, I was still operating as a Type A with Type T inclinations but no experience operating at that level. So I entered with guns not quite a-blazing, but definitely visible. The HR department was clearly not aligned with the core values of the company, two of which were: "Our employees are our greatest asset," and " delighting the customer."

Think back to the company whose HR door was locked, with a sign that said, "Closed. Open 10-2." The greatest assets in the company were allowed to be delighted with internal customer service if, and only if, they could get there between 10 and 2, which, even then, was marginal at best. When asked why the door was locked and the available hours were limited, I was told they had work to do and needed quiet time. Unfortunately, the team didn't make the connection between serving the internal customers and valuing employees and their operational practices.

My vision for the department was a little different than what I encountered. My philosophy had always been that HR's role was to design and deliver products and services to meet the customer's needs, when they needed them. The "customer" included all employees and internal and external constituencies, and HR staff was expected to model and be an example of excellent customer service and the core values for other employees.

You May Be Getting in Your Own Way

To say that there was limited buy-in to my vision is an understatement. Not only was it limited, but there was subtle sabotage to most initiatives. There were regular leaks in confidentiality, and it was a matter of minutes before sensitive issues were being gossiped about throughout the company. There was a total lack of trust and professionalism in the staff of the department, but, on the surface, they were charming and appeared supportive. Behind the scenes, there were several moles and snakes, who intimidated others in the department and encouraged them to resist any of my initiatives.

Then one brave soul in the department, who was not in a management position and about three levels down the organizational chart from my position, asked if we could meet after work for a beer. When we met, she said she was about to make a potentially career-limiting move, but she trusted me and wanted to see me succeed. I had no idea where the conversation was going.

She proceeded to explain that she was aligned with my goals and vision, and a few of the other team members were too, but they were being coerced to resist. She also told me that if I approached things a little differently, I might get less resistance. Upon my request for guidance, she proceeded to give examples and alternatives. She was spot-on with her recommendations. My residual Type A approach to dealing with people and solving problems was interfering with getting the results I really wanted.

This was one brave woman to tell the vice president of her department that her leadership style was getting in the way of achieving the desired results. I had huge admiration for this woman for her guts, compassion and excellent advice.

Her advice had more to do with the delivery of my communication than the message. That was before I had studied the concepts about the impact of vibrational energy on effective communication. So I'm sure when I was dealing with my resistant and passive-aggressive management team, my vibes were reflecting my underlying thoughts, which were probably nasty. But I think I had a Type T, intuitive sense that I needed to align my thinking to all that I wanted for a healthy and productive environment and focus less on their toxic behavior.

A Two-Pronged Approach to Accountability

We started a department book discussion on a popular book at the time, *The Customer Comes Second* by Hal Rosenbluth and Diane McFerrin Peters. The book focused on creating a culture of internal service for employees so that outstanding service could be provided externally to customers, suppliers and shareholders. Half of the group loved the book discussion, and the other half hated it. It was then that I knew who was on the team and who wasn't. Basically, the people who wanted to complain and keep doing the same mediocre work hated the book and resisted the idea of creating a culture of service and accountability. The people who were on board with the future direction of the department embraced the ideas and started implementing some of them. They were engaged in ways to enhance not only the services provided, but the image of the department.

I took a two-pronged approach to improve internal customer service and create a culture of accountability. One was through department meetings with group updates and the book discussions. I also continued to have individual meetings that focused on job duties, project status and performance, as compared to goals and plans. There was one major initiative for a performance management system that required three managers to collaborate and coordinate the design and implementation. Deadlines were set by each person, missed and reset. Missed and reset. We discussed, individually and as a team, what tools, resources and assistance were needed to help them accomplish their goals. Having implemented a system similar to this in a previous company, I understood the complexity and offered assistance, and they assured me none was needed. But I knew that nothing was being done, and they really didn't know what they were doing, based on their answers to my questions. So, I just held them accountable to the tasks and deadlines that they set for themselves and the project team. This approach made them very uncomfortable because no one had ever held these managers accountable before, particularly to the goals they set for themselves.

Then, one night a manager came to my office after hours, crying and fessing up to the fact that they had no idea what they were doing and needed help. Finally. I thanked her for her honesty and request for assistance and told her I'd be delighted to walk them through the process so they could learn how to design, develop and implement the system successfully. At first, the other managers were furious and felt betrayed by her for exposing their little lie. But the pressure of being accountable for meeting their own goals and deadlines was too much to bear.

Have Confidence in Your Authenticity and Integrity

The point is that leaders who are modeling or changing their leadership style to a Type T style of leadership can make people uncomfortable. The transformational leader is more transparent, more authentic, and, in some ways, more vulnerable than a Type A leader. People are generally not used to this approach and can respond with suspiciousness and skepticism, especially if they have never been held accountable to a higher standard. It's normal to encounter resistance. The key is to stay focused, communicate the vision and model the way of authenticity and integrity. Be persistent and consistent in modeling the key words that you've chosen for who you are as a leader. Share expectations and ask how they can engage in the process. Always remember that people have a choice, whether to engage or not when expectations and accountabilities are clear and consistent. It then becomes their choice as to the level of their participation and commitment.

Sometimes, sharing the vision and involving people in the process is beyond a person's capacity. Many people at the lower levels of work performance would prefer to be told what to do. There is no desire for ownership or participation. They may glaze over when you talk about the big picture or the vision and even say, "Just tell me what to do." In situations like that, you then have two choices, tell them what to do and do not expect buy-in, participation or commitment or encourage them to find another position, which is ultimately the best solution.

What I've found over the years is that most people who choose not to participate at the desired level or rise to the accountabilities and expectations will "deselect," just as it was described at the rural hospital. They will find another position internally that is a better fit, with more structure and direction or they will leave the organization.

It's at that point that you honor them and what they have contributed to date, wish them well and send them on their way.

Leading A, B and C Employees

You will find through your Type T performance management process that you will have A, B and C members on your team. The best way to describe the A, B and C team members is to apply the analogy that we used when starting a corporate wellness program. When embarking on a comprehensive corporate wellness program, we realized there were three tiers of people as it related to their well being. There were A's. They generally ate healthy foods, exercised, and if they drank, it was limited or in moderation, and they didn't smoke. The B's were moderately healthy—they had areas for improvement, such as a better exercise program, quitting smoking or reducing processed foods. The C's were the smokers, ate high-calorie, fatty foods or fast food regularly, didn't exercise and were not inclined to care about their immediate or long-term health.

The goal of the wellness program was to focus on the A's and B's. Support the A's with healthy options and choices; help the B's move to A, or at least stay at B and prevent them from becoming C's. Not a lot of time and energy was spent in developing programs or trying to reform the C's. In fact, I remember being asked if the wellness program would get a specific individual who was a four-pack-a-day smoker to quit. My response was yes—if he truly wanted to quit, which was doubtful, and suggested that his quitting smoking really shouldn't be a measure of the program's success.

The same holds true for performance management. So often the squeaky wheel gets the grease. When, in fact, effective Type T leaders will provide tools, options and resources for the C's, but if they don't take advantage of it, that's their choice. The Type T leader is focused on helping the A performers stay at their peak and expand their skills and with coaching the B performers by providing feedback and opportunities that motivate and help them develop their skills. Not every person can be a rock star or an A player either. Sometimes, they are almost as demanding as the C's. Paying the right amount of attention to the steady performer can reap great rewards for the whole team. Oftentimes, I will ask organizational leaders what it would be like if every person simply "met expectations." Their response is usually that it would be fantastic if every person performed his or her job by meeting the expectations of the position. Why spend inordinate amounts of time and energy on the marginal performers? Hold people accountable to do the job for which they are being paid. Reward them for consistency and give greater rewards to the people who consistently exceed expectations.

The authentic, transformational leader is managing and coaching individuals and the team to higher levels of commitment and performance. Using the vision and values as the connecting factors, people will feel aligned and accountable for the team and organizational success. As the team and individuals gain success and the leader relinquishes control, others can take ownership, and they will start to operate at a higher level whether the leader is there or not. In team meetings, they will hold each other accountable for fulfilling commitments and demonstrating the values.

By reinforcing and celebrating milestones and accomplishments, teams will transform beyond average performance, and people will know that there's something different happening in that department or in that company. It will attract the people who want to be aligned with that kind of culture and that kind of vision and transformation. When in the corporate world, as the vice president of human resources, I saw in each company I worked where people would literally take pay cuts to work in a department with that kind of culture and opportunities to grow and contribute. I had several employees in different companies who took $10,000 to $20,000 reductions in pay in order to create a new career path in human resources and work in a healthier, more productive culture. For most of these people, they have gone on to become senior managers and vice presidents at other companies.

The bottom line is that some team members will want to be part of transforming a culture and standards of performance, and some won't. But if you lay out the opportunities, then they get to choose. They can then take accountability for their future, their growth and development and their best expression of their skills and abilities. It becomes their choice, not yours.

Chapter 17

The Power of Courageous Collaboration

Collaboration is becoming a more trendy term these days, perhaps because we have seen so little of it in our communities nationally and internationally. We haven't had many role models for true collaboration, so let's start with some basics.

The Merriam Webster definition is, "to work with another person or group in order to achieve or do something."

I happen to like Wikipedia's definition better: "Collaboration is working with each other to do a task and to achieve shared goals. It's where two or more people or organizations work together to realize shared goals, by sharing knowledge, learning and building consensus." Most collaboration requires leadership. In particular, teams that work collaboratively can obtain greater resources, recognition and reward when facing competition for finite resources

I see collaboration as more than the traditional model of "win-win." In that model, it always seemed that, although we'd say it's a win-win, someone always felt like they had lost something. They had to give up something or the compromise left someone feeling like they got the short end of the stick.

I see true collaboration as an approach that considers all components and looking at the big picture, rather than individual wants and desires. Collaborative, Type T leaders guide the process, and there is a willingness to share resources, ideas and goals for the greater good because the whole is greater than the sum of its parts.

An example of true collaboration comes from a pretty unlikely source, at least on the surface: Lady Gaga, the popular singer who emerged on the music scene in the United States in 2008. In 2009, the number one CD in the country was by Susan Boyle. Remember her? The Scottish woman who blew people away with her beautiful voice and plain appearance and won Britain's Got Talent competition? While Susan Boyle had the number one CD that year, Lady Gaga had 322 million music downloads on the Internet the same year. Susan Boyle had 133,000 downloads of her music over the same timespan.

Lady Gaga, an astute businesswoman at the age of 24, saw the future, which was downloading music, not buying CDs. She saw that record labels would go out of business at this rate. So she resurrected an old model used in the music business called "The 360 Deal." Under this arrangement, the recording companies promote the artist upfront for tours around the world. In return, they receive a percentage of sales on the back end, for all ticket sales and merchandise sales. This was the model that Lady Gaga used.

So who wins? Everyone! Lady Gaga is promoted and booked around the world to sellout crowds, the record label wins because they receive a percentage of revenue from ticket and merchandise sales and, we, as consumers, win because we can still download music for a fraction of the cost of buying a CD.

This is courageous collaboration at its best.

Courageous collaboration is stepping outside of the known or established models that no longer work effectively. It is an opportunity to share goals and objectives, share resources and make choices that are for the good of all. Everyone wins.

Earlier I mentioned facilitating a conference roundtable discussion on "courageous collaboration." As I said, people could choose from a variety of sessions or roundtable discussions on different business topics, so I was curious why they chose to attend this roundtable and what they wanted to discuss about this topic. Some of the actual responses I heard included:

- I want to figure out how to get people to do what I want.
- I want to influence people.
- I want to be heard, to have people listen to what I have to say.

Do you see a trend here? "I want, I want, I want . . ." Interestingly, the topic was courageous collaboration, yet these responses had little to do with courage or collaboration. Even so, this small group of intellectually curious seekers stayed for the conversation.

By the end of the roundtable discussion, it became clear to the group at the table that collaboration had nothing to do with individual wants or needs. They saw that collaboration was achieved by active listening and questioning, authentic interest about the other person's needs and goals and genuine interest in seeking common ground.

It was fascinating to watch the faces of the participants as the light bulbs went on, and they discovered that to get what they wanted meant giving up control of the outcomes. It meant giving up control of "telling" and being open to asking questions, being willing to hear options, ideas, and caring as much about others' needs and goals, as much as their own.

It sounds so very simple, yet we are trained to "look out for #1!" This approach does not come naturally. Type T's, however, strive to look out for the good of the whole.

Sources of Power and Building Collaborative Relationships

When people approach a situation with the intent to look out for themselves and their own best interests, it can breed distrust. There's a scarcity mentality. It's as if people feel they have to protect themselves and their little fiefdoms, lest someone wants to take away any power that they have—power in the form of resources, information or personal power.

One of the greatest sources of power, however, is information. If you are truly interested in collaboration, that means you must be willing to share information, share resources and give up controlling everything you know or have or want. You have to be willing to give up controlling other people too!

Trust is inherent in collaboration. I'm not suggesting that you be naïve in your negotiations, especially with people you do not have an established relationship with. On the contrary, collaboration comes from building relationships and establishing shared goals as a means to create a bigger piece of the pie for everyone.

Cavett Robert, founder of the National Speakers Association, started the organization so professional speakers could "stand on the shoulders of others" to achieve success. His belief was that people should not fight for a piece of the pie, but "work to create a bigger pie." He started the organization with that philosophy and 40 years later, the organization continues to promote collaboration, camaraderie and professional development to create a bigger pie.

A non-speaker friend of mine once asked me why I belong to an organization and socialized and brainstormed with "competitors." Being a competitive Type A kind of gal, the idea of hanging out with competitors was a foreign concept to her and actually seemed like a stupid thing to do. I tried to explain that we don't view ourselves as competitors and even if our subject matter may seem the same on the surface, our styles and approaches are dramatically different. Some clients love my approach and style and others don't. We readily refer business to each other if we're booked or if the fit isn't right for the client.

However, it is important to note that these collaborative relationships didn't just happen overnight. Reflecting back on the best collaborative relationships with my speaker buddies, it's taken several years of building friendships, shared ideas, volunteering together and seeing how each other operates in volunteer situations. Can we count on each other? Do we honor commitments? Do we respect each other's time and talent? Establishing relationships in a volunteer setting is a great way to really know if you can trust another person and collaborate with each other's best interests in mind.

There are people who are takers, and there people who are givers. We've seen them all before. When people have a mentality of scarcity, they're more interested in protecting themselves and promoting their own self-interests. It's very hard to collaborate with a "taker." They're usually afraid of getting the short end of the stick and making sure they get what they want. The level of trust is limited.

Collaboration Is a Mindset

Living a life of collaboration is an ongoing endeavor and not always easy. Living life in a collaborative manner can't be restricted to just one area of your life, either. It's not like you can say, "I'll be collaborative with my family and not with coworkers." Collaboration is a mindset. And it is a mindset that can be developed and nurtured. This is what the Type T leader does.

Living a life of collaboration is not a one-time deal either. I encountered an interesting situation when I was facilitating a workshop on raising the bar on performance for a group of highly successful mortgage loan officers. The topic of courageous collaboration was presented and was under discussion with the group. Keep in mind that these loan officers were commission-only salespeople. They competed with each other and anyone who crossed their paths. The concept of collaboration was clearly not on their radar screen and certainly nothing they thought could be of value to them. Their boss, being a transformational leader, was very interested in them learning the benefits of collaboration, as a means to increase performance, profitability and overall well being.

There was a young woman in the room whose production and income had dipped slightly the previous month due to changing market conditions. The day before the workshop, she advised her boss that she thought *he* should terminate her assistant because she "couldn't afford to keep him on as her assistant" if slower market conditions continued. The reality was that she could afford to keep him as her assistant; she was just being greedy. She wanted to keep her share of the pie. The manager declined and told her that just because sales had slipped slightly, it was not appropriate to terminate someone on a whim, and if she chose to terminate him, she would be the one to deliver the message. She did not like this response.

During the workshop, we were discussing the elements of collaboration and why it is important to consider making decisions that are for the good of the whole. At this point, the young woman asked if this information was to be applied on that day during the workshop. Basically, she was asking when and how long do I need to collaborate with these people.

I told her that, yes, it was to be applied that day, with her colleagues—and every day with her colleagues, with the underwriters, with the processors and closers . . . and the intention was that she also applied the concepts of collaboration with her family, her friends, her neighbors, her spiritual community, her kids' teachers and school . . .

On that note, you could hear a pin drop. Her jaw dropped and face sagged. There was a collective sigh in the room. Collaborating with people all the time was clearly a daunting thought.

As the workshop continued, people began to see not only the benefits of a collective spirit, but the room became lighter, more joyous, more inspired and more productive. By the end of the day, the group was committed to the grand experiment of achieving results though collaboration.

They began to understand that a collaborative mindset is intentional. It is deliberate. Thoughts, words and actions need to be aligned with looking out for the good of the whole, working together for a common goal. Even though they were commission-only salespeople, they needed to rely on others to be successful.

The manager of the group called me two days later with some very exciting news. The young woman who resisted the idea of collaboration had not only acknowledged her selfishness in wanting to terminate her assistant, she had declared a new attitude and commitment to her work and to focus on collaborating with others to achieve sales success. Within one day of her declaration, she closed a sale for over $1 million dollars, the largest sale she'd ever had. She felt that this accomplishment was directly related to having a different mindset when she worked with the client.

And, the manager reported that there was more good news as a result of the workshop. Three regional managers created a "game" for their commission-only loan officers to get required paperwork completed and submitted to the corporate office, not only on time, but completed 100% by 100% of the team. They assigned points and rewards for the accurate and timely completion of reports. But the profound difference was that people would not receive the reward unless every person on the team completed the reports 100% accurately and 100% on time. Now, the loan officers had a stake in the game if their colleagues didn't comply. Peer pressure prompted the group to work together to achieve a collective reward. The corporate office began to see a trend of reports being filed on time and accurately, which had never happened before, by any office. The game was fun and a great example of "everyone winning."

It was a "Professor Higgins" moment, like in the movie *My Fair Lady*, when he declared, "I think she's got it! By Jove, I think she's got it!" The branch manager and I were so proud of the group for taking the concepts, applying them immediately and seeing the benefits and results. What seemed like an airy-fairy concept to them at first had become very real, and they saw both the financial and personal rewards of collaboration.

So the point of this story is that at work, the Type T leader will align people and processes so that all departments are working together. Infighting and territorial behaviors are replaced with an understanding and appreciation for the value of what each area contributes and how important each is to the success of the whole process.

Collaboration in Rural Kenya

As described in an earlier chapter, I had the opportunity to spend time with some community leaders in rural Kenya, which is where I witnessed exquisite and humbling examples of collaboration. It is said that rural Kenya is a group society and decisions are made with the best interest of the community in mind.

Imagine going to an area so rural, it was only identified by its GPS coordinates when registering with the State Department before the trip. Picture meeting the community leaders in their homes, which did not have indoor plumbing or electricity. Imagine meeting the women who were the community leaders who carried 50 - 75 pounds of water, on their heads, five times a day for a quarter to a half mile each.

"Mama Jane" was one of these women, who started leading a small community of about 12 - 20 people to pool resources for farming their land and taking produce to the market. She explained that, over the years, the group grew to over 500, and she was the treasurer for the community. This community now functioned like a co-op and a credit union for the group because the country's banks charged over 25%- 30% interest for loans.

Mama Jane explained their decision-making process, which is to do what is best for the whole community. When pooling resources, dispersing profits, making loans and investing in resources for the community, she said all decisions were made collectively and for the good of the group of 600 people. We asked her what they did if someone was being selfish and wanted something that would not benefit the whole group. She said, "We keep talking until they understand."

We insisted, and asked again: what do you do if someone wants his or her own way?

We keep talking, she said.

Remember the Blessing Stick carried by the elders and representative of their wisdom? It was passed to anyone not listening, only wanting his or her own way, and that person had to hold it as a reminder not to be self-serving, to act on the behalf of the community. And there the Blessing Stick stayed, until the person was able to make the group and the community the priority.

In the face of what we would call poverty, here are groups of people and large communities, sharing resources and making decisions and choices so everyone wins, no matter how meager those resources may be. Their hearts were open to us, and they welcomed us into their homes and their hearts. The leaders of each group we met would say, "We welcome you. We honor you. We love you. You always have a home with us."

Humbling and exquisite simplicity.

Imagine a World of Collaboration and Pay-It-Forward

Imagine the outcomes if we put aside our need for more "stuff," more status, more control and started welcoming and honoring our friends and neighbors more. Imagine the outcomes if husbands and wives collaborated and taught their kids the importance of accountability and making choices that are for the good of the whole family, including stepparents, and stepbrothers and sisters, in-laws, grandparents and cousins. When families learn and practice true collaboration, they will be healthier, happier and able to make greater contributions to each other and their communities. Now extend that to organizations and imagine the same impact there.

This "pay-it-forward" attitude will be carried forward—one person at a time. The spirit of courageous collaboration can start with just one person, practicing collaboration at home with family members or at work with colleagues, customers and suppliers. Imagine how contagious the collaborative spirit could be, if just one person created the intention and made the commitment to start being more collaborative. The Type T leader knows that it only takes that one person to start the movement, whether it's community, family or work team.

Type A people will be more likely to have a wait-and-see attitude. They will take action to be collaborative only if others do it first. They don't want to risk being the only one. Type T leaders know it's up to them to be the role model and lead the way.

Again, as with the ways to developing and incorporating a new vision and representative key words, a person who demonstrates a collaborative spirit consistently learns to do so by asking:

- What would I be saying if I were being collaborative?
- What would I be doing if I were acting in a more collaborative manner?
- What would my organization, community or family look and sound like if we were acting with each other's best interest at heart?
- What would we be doing if we were looking out for the good of the whole?
- Most importantly, what difference would this make to our quality of life?

Right now you're probably thinking—I want that! Wouldn't it be wonderful?

Then, immediately, reality sets in and the fears and barriers crop up that might prevent you from taking actions that are aligned with the collaborative spirit.

"Other people will think I'm crazy. They'll think I'm a dreamer and unrealistic. It could never happen."

Yes. There will be people who say that, and they are not the ones you need to convince or try to change. There will also be people who think it's risky to collaborate and to being open to considering other points of view. Again, this is a scarcity, fear-based mentality. It is fear of the unknown and fear of losing control that may be driving them to hold on so tightly.

So my question is: What would happen if you gave up trying to control outcomes or trying to control other people?

Giving up control is not about being "weak" or undecided. Unfortunately, many of the people in positions of perceived power and influence have this viewpoint. These so-called role models use their power to manipulate, dominate and control outcomes, usually for their own self-serving interests.

I invite you to take The Two Week Challenge to give up trying to control outcomes, to collaborate with the best interest of the whole in mind. How would your life be different? How would the lives of those close to you be different?

It's worth a try.

Type T:
Living The New Normal

Chapter 18

The Multigenerational Workplace

An important factor that enlightened leaders are starting to encounter is grooming the current workforce for higher-level positions, specifically Generation Y or Millennials, as they are sometimes called, who were born between approximately 1980 and 2000. NBC News reported that there has been a shift in the U.S. population: for the first time since 1947, the biggest age group isn't Baby Boomers; it's Millennials. They make up about 30% of the workforce and by 2020 will be about 50% of the workforce. Baby Boomers, representing 35 - 40% of the workforce, are starting to retire or create new or part-time positions to reflect the lifestyles they want or to supplement their incomes.

Generation X, born between 1965 - 1980, represents about 30% of the population. And the "Veterans" or "Silent" generation are those born between 1922 - 1945, representing about 10% of the workforce.

Due to the Great Recession, starting in 2008 and running through 2013, many people who were established in the workplace lost jobs, and the Gen Y's have found it harder to get a job. Baby Boomers started turning 65, and yet, many have been reluctant or unable to retire. Reluctant because they want to continue to work and contribute or unable because they lost significant amounts of money allocated for retirement (or simply have not saved enough to retire). So the workforce is clogged with four generations, each competing to obtain or retain a job and each generation with vastly different values and skills to contribute. And it won't be long before the Gen Z's (born after 2000) will be entering the workforce and some already are!

Let's take a look at some key factors of each generation and what makes them tick because the transformational leader will tap into these attributes to assure each person is able to contribute his or her skills and abilities to the needs of the organization.

The Veterans or Silent Generation

The Veterans or Silent Generation, while a small portion in the workforce, are the legacy of many organizations. They may be figureheads, a guiding force or, in some cases, they may be a barrier to the organization moving forward and toward greater financial success and sustainability. The people in this generation were shaped by the end of The Depression era, World War II and the Korean War. They were raised believing that sacrifice, dedication, conformity and discipline are important work values. They believe in hard work and take a "command and control" style of management. In addition, they are more formal and believe in being directive and structured. Security is important.

The Baby Boomers

Ken Dychtwald, CEO of Age Wave, discusses the impact of this generation from the time they were infants to current day because of the sheer number of people in this generation. As the Boomers age, so goes the nation. This generation was raised during the Viet Nam War, Civil Rights and Women's Movements and believed they could change the world—and they did. As leaders, they were less "command and control" and more consensual and collegial, more team oriented and vision driven. They were often workaholics and driven by "causes" but truly enjoyed money, titles and visible signs of success.

Generation X

The X generation, 30% of the population, is very much of a sandwich generation, caught between the aging and dominant Baby Boomers and the Millennials, who seem to demand special attention in a whole different way.

The X'ers were the latchkey kids. Their mothers were in the workforce, many in high earning positions and/or as a single parent working two or possibly three jobs to support the family. This generation had to be self-reliant at an early age. They were also impacted in their early years by growing up in a fairly robust economy. Then things dramatically changed, and many saw the effects of corporate downsizings that impacted their families. Having to be self-reliant and competent at an early age, many tended to be entrepreneurial and autonomous as leaders. They had to be more flexible than previous generations and have a tendency to be less formal and more results oriented.

Generation Y

The Millenials are now entering the workforce and represent values and ideals that are very foreign to the Baby Boomers, in particular. I find this somewhat amazing because the Boomers and older X'ers are the ones who raised this generation and taught them everything they know. They were raised to believe that they were "special," most notably that every kid got a trophy for showing up and were rarely told "no." They had computers at an early age and communicate through instant messaging, text and social media. Email and voice mails are often unopened or unacknowledged.

They expect immediate and positive feedback and want meaningful work. Generally, they are adept at multitasking and are accustomed to working in groups or teams, so collaboration comes more easily to them. Some say this generation can represent the best of the previous three. They hold the philanthropic or service philosophy of the Veterans, the visionary and democratic style of the Boomers and the flexibility and autonomy of the X'ers.

The Y's Have Reshaped the World

Just as 2008 was a watershed year in terms of redefining how we operate and how we think, the Millennials are making their mark in the workforce. So, it's important to look a little deeper to see what makes them tick and how we need to adapt and adjust to not only the new economy, but to the people who will be running the economy in the decades ahead.

This generation was raised to be connected 24/7. They only know a global society, and they only know a digitized world. Texting the person next to them is commonplace, rather than speaking to them. Since many were coddled and nurtured their whole lives, many parents and extended family members made sure they only knew success and had a strong sense of self-esteem. Learning via hard knocks was the exception, not the norm. Teachers were sometimes advised not to use red ink to correct papers because it hurt the students' feelings to be criticized or told they made a mistake. Parents wanted to protect their kids from any potential or perceived danger or threat. On the flip side, parents had more cause for worries in that regard than previous generations, as there has been more inherent danger in the classrooms, starting with Columbine and the massive tragedy at Sandy Hook elementary school. Parents did have more cause for worries and concerns about the safety of their children than ever before, not only at school, but also from the general violence in their communities, at malls, movie theatres and even public zoos.

These kids were pampered in many ways because the parents wanted to be sure they didn't lack for anything. They had scheduled and supervised activities from sunrise to sunset, piano, soccer, ballet, archery, karate, Spanish.

More parents were actively involved in their kids' education, often advising teachers how to do their jobs. "Helicopter" parents hovered as they selected classes at colleges, roommates and dorm rooms. Some parents intervened and protested when their kid received a lower grade than the parents thought they deserved, or God forbid, failed a class.

Since parents so actively managed activities, schedules and choices, many of the Millennials lacked fundamental decision-making skills, making them ill-equipped to make mature choices without parental advice or close supervision and guidance from a supervisor or mentor.

Now, some good news about this generation. Overall, they are adept at technology and inquisitive about how things work. They know how to navigate the digital, global world through technology and connect with people in dramatically different ways than the Baby Boomers. Because they grew up in groups and structured activities, there's a level of teamwork, participation, collaboration and sociability that will be an attribute in the workplace. And, despite the negative aspects of "a trophy for everyone," this generation has a sense of confidence and achievement that, when coached and guided in the workplace, will be valuable.

In addition, this generation strives for work/life balance. Unlike the Boomers who worked 50, 60, 70 hours a week to get ahead at all costs, it's not unusual for a Gen Y employee to take a lower-paying job to have more free time or leave a job to travel. Because they grew up with interracial and multiple ethnicities in school, they are more comfortable with diversity than previous generations. Given that we're a global society, these are skills and attitudes that can make a huge difference for an organization. Plus, they have been accused of wanting work to be fun! For older generations in a bottom-line world, there's no room for fun! Imagine, fun in a bottom-line world! Millennials don't see this as an either/or proposition, as previous generations have.

I met a 29-year-old man who worked in the aerospace industry. He explained that he took another position that had less prestige because he wanted to have experience supervising people. The unit he supervised was considered a place for people "who couldn't do anything else." It was manual labor work, and the people were said to have bad attitudes. His colleagues scoffed at him for taking that position.

After 18 months, he said that unit was "the place people wanted to work." He said, "We laughed every day. I loved them and cared about them and their families. They became proud of their work."

This young man knew that work can be fun, and people work better when they know someone cares. It makes me wonder if the Millennials will be Type T leaders faster than any other generation.

The Millennials hold similar values to the Silent Generation in their desire to serve their community and engage in more philanthropic endeavors.

While these are admittedly broad generalizations of each generation, there is truth in them, so let's take a look at how the Type T leader can incorporate this information to create a healthy, productive and profitable work environment.

Clear and Complete Communication

The role of the transformational leader in communicating effectively, especially with the Millennials, will require skill and patience.

Many Millennials have been raised in a nonverbal, isolated environment. Even when there are other people around, Gen Y's can be found heads down, texting or looking up information on their mobile devices, rather than talking or asking others for information. Their face-to-face verbal interaction and social skills may be more limited than the previous generations. Consider how many students are home-schooled or choose to be educated online, missing the diversity of others and/or adapting to other human beings in real time. Speaking in complete sentences, not 140 characters, developing coherent, well thought-out viewpoints, both verbally and in writing, and listening to others are not skills that have been encouraged or expected.

Many Millennials lament about having to listen to their Baby Boomer bosses "drone on" about the past or the history of a project or background information about a client. Millennials have said, "What does this have to do with me? This isn't important to know." What the Type T leader understands is that, many times, the background information is important, and their role is to coach and educate the Gen Y's that not everything has to do with them and that the droning on of the past or history is, in many ways, providing context for decision making.

Millennials need to be trained in decision making that is more than a checklist or algorithm of "if/then" statements. In many situations, decisions have an emotional component that needs to be considered and that can only be learned via an understanding of past experiences. On the other hand, Boomers may need to be reminded that they can't dwell in the past, need to get to the point, make content relevant and connect the dots so people see and understand the matrix world of decision making.

Many times Millennials, in their effort to expedite tasks and check off items from the list, overlook the ramifications and interconnectedness of their work to others, especially to the customer. When I was working with a social media firm that employed people between the ages of 20 - 28, I was appalled by their lack of understanding about the importance of quality work and quality service. This, combined with their lack of business experience and lack of desire to understanding the flow and impact of work processes, was horrifying.

The task of writing content for my website or blogs was excruciating and required extensive rewrites and editing on my part. I explained that I understood there would be a learning curve, as it related to understanding my work and being able to write good content, but I expected them to proofread and edit work before sending it to me for review. Over the course of a couple months, it was apparent that no one proofed or edited anything. Spelling errors, missing words, words that didn't belong in the sentence and sentences that didn't make sense were regular occurrences, despite numerous requests to double-check their work before sending it to me. The account reps and writers on my account were changed three times in four months to assure me that quality work was possible and that these experiences were not the norm.

When my website was moved to a new server, no one thought to check what would happen to emails in the transition. I was out of the country and effectively "off the grid" for two weeks and had no idea what was happening nor did my virtual assistant, who covered for me while I was away. When I returned, I found that all emails were essentially lost for more than two weeks—into oblivion and cyberspace—never to be found or retrieved. Their response was "Oh." Not, "I'm so sorry; we'll do whatever we can to help you . . ."

Information sent to them was repeatedly lost, and they would request that I resend documents. Growing up in a digital world, they thought it was easier for me to locate and resend information than look for it themselves. I finally refused to resend information and told them they had to find it. I was not willing to correct their incompetence or tolerate their laziness. Somehow they found this approach insulting.

Since many Millennials were trained that they were special and didn't make mistakes, or that it's ok to fail as long as they tried, apologies do not come easily or naturally. This can be very annoying to someone who expects, and is paying for, good quality work and good service.

Lest you think it was an isolated case and I just happened to hire a poorly run company, the trend for these kinds of work habits are not restricted to this one firm. I was engaged to speak about business professionalism to a group of "emerging professionals" at a networking event. This was a group of people who work at a variety of organizations and are between the ages of 20 - 35. When I saw the draft of the meeting announcement, I requested that they change the wording and refer to me as "Marty," not by my last name, as in: "Stanley will be speaking about . . ." When the actual notice was sent, they changed my name in one place, but I was referred to as "Stanley" three more times in the body of the message.

I contacted the meeting planner, who was 24 years old, and pointed out that the changes had not been made. During our discussion, he expressed great embarrassment and confessed that he didn't read the whole message and only corrected the first sentence. While we joked and laughed how this can happen when we're rushed, we talked about how this incident was, in essence, an example of the business professionalism that emerging professionals need to learn if they are to succeed in the workplace. He was a good sport and readily shared it with the group as a valuable learning experience.

Type T leaders will be working with and encountering the quirkiness of the Millennials and needing to blend the talents they bring to the workplace with their frequent one-dimensional, self-oriented interpersonal skills

While this may sound overly critical of this generation, we need to remember that we are living in a global society where goods and services can be purchased anywhere, any time. The Program for International Student Assessment, or PISA, collects test results from 65 countries for its rankings in science, mathematics and reading. The results, reported in 2012, show that U.S. students rank #29 in math, #23 in science and #20 in reading among 65 of the world's most-developed countries. The top overall scores came from Shanghai, Singapore, Hong Kong, Taiwan, South Korea, Macao and Japan, followed by Lichtenstein, Switzerland, the Netherlands and Estonia. If we are to be a competitive nation, we cannot tolerate poor performance, sloppy work and incomplete communication—regardless of age and regardless of technical prowess. Successful organizations will still require people to read and write and to build healthy, productive relationships and high quality products and services.

Chapter 19

Workplace of the Future

Given that there may be four generations in the workplace, compensation, benefits, job design and human resource policies and practices can no longer be "cookie-cutter." Some say there are really *five* generations at work: Gen Z—those born after 2000 are starting in summer jobs or jobs appropriate for young teens. There can no longer be a one-size-fits-all, take-it-or-leave-it approach to attracting and retaining key talent.

Benefit packages and job design need to be flexible to meet the needs of people in their 20's and 30's, as well as 50's and 60's and possibly 70's. One thing that the Millennials and Boomers have in common is that they value time off. Many Millennials have said that if given the choice of a high-paying job that would rquire more time at work and less time with friends and family, they would choose having more free time. Boomers, many of whom worked 60+ hours a week during the heights of their careers, want to continue to work, but want free time as well.

So the 8am - 5pm, 40 hour work week is no longer relevant or of interest to many in the workforce. And it's compounded by the fact that many organizations are serving customers or constituents in multiple time zones.

Flextime, job sharing and telecommuting will become the norm, to not only attract the right people to do the work, but to meet the needs of customers. Inherent in this, but often overlooked, is having the right training and monitoring structures to ensure success. Many traditional managers and supervisors think that they need to see people at work, at their desks, to be sure they are performing. This attitude is more prevalent in seasoned (aka older) managers, not accustomed to a virtual environment. And many people think they should be able to work from home and have flexible hours, just because it would be more convenient—for them.

People, both managers and employees, will need to have clear expectations about job duties and performance. Key performance indicators, measures and monitors will need to be established, communicated and agreed upon to guarantee success. As an organization starts to introduce alternative work arrangements, it's a good idea to start with higher-performing employees, your A and B people. Definitely do not offer flexible arrangements to your C people because, if they are having trouble performing and meeting expectations in a traditional work environment, chances are they will not succeed in a virtual environment that is more self-driven and requires more self-discipline and accountability. Trust between both parties is essential. Typically the manager's thought is "How can I trust them to really be working if I can't see them?" That's why trust and key performance indicators and tools to measure and monitor work are needed for everyone's benefit.

Quality, quantity, service levels, error rates, rework and expectations for communication should all be considered before starting flexible work arrangements. Too often employees and managers jump into a virtual work arrangement, only to find that a lot of things fall through the cracks because the implementation was not well planned.

It's been said that for every hour spent in planning, that you will save three in implementation. Frankly, in complex, matrix and cross-functional work environments, I think advance planning will save more than three hours in implementation—perhaps six or seven hours because of the rework, reviewing and repeating expectations and clearing up misunderstandings that result from poor or late planning.

So, when considering different job designs for a more virtual environment, it's imperative to think it through thoroughly and plan the workflow from start to finish, taking into consideration the needs and expectations of the end user and the internal and external customers. What structures and systems need to be in place for communication and workflow to assure a smooth process?

It bears repeating that Type T's know that traditional benefit packages will need to be reviewed and updated to reflect the demographics of the current and future desired workforce. The nature of insurance benefits is changing rapidly and traditional insurance plans will no longer work or, in some cases, be affordable for either the employer or employee or both. As the Baby Boomers age and remain in the workplace, Social Security and Medicare benefits will have an impact on both insurance and compensation levels.

Expectations for vacation benefits and time-off policies will come under scrutiny. Most benefits, including corporate and government-sponsored benefits, were established when the life expectancy of most people was under age 65. Ken Dychtwald, of Age Wave, talks about how the traditional model of the aging process, when life expectancy was about 65, used to be, "Education, marriage/family and work/career, maybe take a couple vacations, retire and take a vacation and die."

The average life expectancy is closer to 80 and older, people are working longer and the younger generation's expectations of work are so different that Dychtwald says the life cycle process may look more like this: "Education, work, vacation, family, education, sabbatical, work, vacation, work, sabbatical . . ."

People will continue to grow and change not just jobs, but whole careers throughout their lifetimes. There will be time off to continue studies or do philanthropic work around the world. Organizations will need to have the right benefit structures to adapt to the changing expectations of the workforce. In the United States, vacation practices are among the most meager around the world. European countries offer four to six weeks per year as part of employment packages, and people not only plan to take that time off, but employers expect them to take it. In America, somehow, it's become a badge of honor to deny oneself time off, accumulate vacation time and carry over to the next year, only to buy back or max-out and lose accumulated time off. Some people view this as a sign of commitment and loyalty. I think it's a sign of stupidity. People need time off to replenish, reflect, rejuvenate and reconnect to the world around them and their families and friends. To explore, to relax, to do what nurtures their creativity and stamina.

Not only is it good for the employee, it can be good for the organization as well to have people away from their jobs. Some industries require people in certain positions to take time off for two consecutive weeks because, in some cases, if there are any shenanigans going on, it will be noticed within two weeks. Creative bookkeeping, mismanagement of people, processes or resources can usually be discovered during this time. As you can see, it can be to everyone's benefit to have people take their earned time off.

Many contemporary, trendy, successful companies think that the gourmet cafeterias, game rooms, "bring your dog to work," free beer and baristas etc. are the way to attract and retain talent. Frankly, I think what most people really want and what the most successful organizations in the future will focus on will be:

- Providing meaningful work.
- Giving timely and constructive feedback.
- Recognizing people for their contributions.
- Creating an environment where people feel like they are part of creating something beneficial and bigger than themselves.
- Providing quality products and services.
- Having a healthy environment.
- Providing benefits that encourage growth and development.

Companies such as Zappos and Google that were cited for their core values are good examples. We might want to refer to "enlightened" companies or companies with a conscience.

I'm particularly fond of Costco for several reasons. They opened a warehouse in an inner-city area near where I live that had high unemployment and limited job opportunities for people in the area. Costco also provides a good wage and benefits for employees, which many retailers do not. Over ten years later, many of the same employees are there, providing great service. Several years ago, Wall Street lowered their rating because they said Costco could have been more profitable if they didn't provide employee benefits, but the leadership team stood firm in their decision. More recently it was reported that they pay employees a significantly higher wage than the minimum wage, many earning about $20 an hour. And their share price increased 38% between 2012-2014. In addition, they have a policy of marking up goods by only 14% over their cost. They pass the savings on to the customer. Many of their locations have skylights, which provide natural lighting and save on electricity. Plus, they sell a hot dog and soft drink for $1.50—the same price as 1985. How can you not love a company like that?

Many smaller or lesser-known companies are adopting these programs or philosophies, such as Tom's of Maine. When Tom's sells a pair of shoes, a pair of shoes is then given to an impoverished child, and when Tom's sells eyewear, part of the profit is used to save or restore the eyesight for people in developing countries. Author Daniel H. Pink described the company's business model as "expressly built for purpose maximization," whereby Tom's is both selling shoes and selling its ideal; creating consumers that are purchasing shoes and also making a purchase that transforms them into benefactors—a company goal if it is not a consumer goal. And don't forget Ben and Jerry's Ice Cream. Here are their core values:

- Our Product Mission drives us to make fantastic ice cream— for its own sake.
- Our Economic Mission asks us to manage our Company for sustainable financial growth.
- Our Social Mission compels us to use our Company in innovative ways to make the world a better place.

While none of these companies are perfect, they strive to make the world a better place. Just because a company has a "take your dog to work" policy or serves good coffee doesn't mean it's a good place to work. It takes a more integrated strategy to be sustainable. The Type T leader understands this and creates alignment of the vision, policies, practices and demographics of the workforce for the future.

Chapter 20

Planning for Success

You've heard it all before:

"By failing to prepare, you are preparing to fail." Benjamin Franklin

"A goal without a plan is just a wish." Antoine de Saint-Exupery

"If you don't know where you are going, you'll end up someplace else." Yogi Berra

It's amazing how many people talk about making plans and never actually do it. Somehow, I think that people are afraid to make plans. What happens if they don't work out? What if people know I made a plan and didn't achieve it?

In 1980, Kansas City Royals third baseman George Brett had a quest to have a consistent batting average of .400. No one had accomplished this feat since legendary second baseman for the Red Sox Ted Williams, in 1941. While Brett hovered around the .400 mark most of the season, he concluded the year batting .390. He had a plan—did he fail?

Hardliners would say yes. He didn't reach his goal. But I wonder what his batting average would have been if he hadn't set his sights on .400 when the previous year, 1979, he batted .329 and in the year before that, in 1978, his average was .278.

One would think that setting goals in an organizational setting would be commonplace. Yet I have worked with many management teams that have been notoriously sluggish about setting goals. One group, in particular, astounded me. One January, I asked each individual on the team if he or she had created resolutions or intentions for the upcoming year, personally or professionally.

Immediately, all heads lowered, eyes avoiding me; they knew what was going to happen next . . . I reminded them that the upcoming year at their organization was going to be extremely challenging. While they already knew that, they didn't see the correlation of setting personal and professional goals as a means of upping their game for the organization. It was like they thought they could run a marathon, without even walking a mile before the big race.

So I asked them to write down one or more personal goals and one or more professional goals for the year.

Right *now?* They asked. Yes. Right now.

I recorded their responses, and each month when I met with them, much to their surprise, they had to report on their progress. You could see each month, as they accomplished some of their goals, that there was a sense of pride in their successes. As a means to visually reinforce this concept, I had them line up facing the wall. I asked them to raise their arms as high as they could and then marked their high point with a post-it note. They stepped back to observe the different levels, based on the various heights of team members. Then I asked them to stand in front of the wall again at their same spot. I asked them to try to increase their previous height by 10% or more. When stepping back this time, they were amazed at how much higher they reached the second time, with just a little more effort.

At this point, they realized that if each person gave just 10% more effort, 10% more intentionality to their work, it would be amazing what could be accomplished. One person admitted not trying very hard the first time, which I think was representative of more than one person in the group. They were being faced with having to increase efficiencies and reduce costs in a short period of time, and they needed to come to work with their A-game in place. But, instead, they were avoiding, blaming and making excuses for their poor performance and lack of goal setting.

Mediocrity is not an option when you are a Type T leader.

At the same time, operating at 100% intensity all of the time isn't an option or even a possibility either. Another organization that I worked with had several major projects that required cross-functional coordination to meet intense deadlines. Everything was a priority, and the intensity never stopped or eased up. It was like the accelerator was pushed to the floor, and people were expected operate at full intensity for months on end. Nothing was ever good enough, and praise or acknowledgement was minimal.

As a transformational leader, finding the right balance is important and will change based on what is going on in your life and work and as circumstances and situations change. To use old measures or old benchmarks for productivity, accomplishments or rejuvenation just won't work. It's important to periodically step back and take note of current conditions and recalibrate expectations and measures of success.

Closing One Year to Plan for the Next

Before we embark on creating your new plans, it's important to put closure to the past. While we have talked about this before, there is a process that I think is valuable to do each year before setting the next year's goals and action plans.

I call it "Closing Out The Year." I do it between Christmas and New Years, often on New Year's Eve. In fact, it's become a rather entailed annual ritual that is all about honoring and acknowledging myself and my accomplishments for the past 12 months. While it may sound self-indulgent, know that no one else will ever acknowledge you for all of the things that you want to be acknowledged for, and no one will do it the way that you want.

I believe that once we learn to "self-acknowledge," other peoples' opinions, acknowledgements or recognition won't be quite as important or critical to our self-esteem or future success.

Doing this annually will provide a depth of reflection that can be worthwhile, rather than if it's only done once or twice. While I use the calendar year end to "close out the year," it can be done any time, such as your birthday or anniversary. Having a specific time is useful as a consistent reminder. Just reflect back on the previous 12 months from whatever time frame you choose.

The Full Ritual

Here's how it works for the full ritual. Plan on spending 5 - 8 hours.

1) Allocate an afternoon and evening to close out the year. Start by spending several hours doing something that you really enjoy. It could be having a long massage, going to an uplifting movie or engaging in a spiritual practice, such as meditation or yoga. For some people, it may be working in the garden, baking something special, taking a long walk or bike ride or an activity that allows you to express yourself artistically. Whatever clears your head and frees your soul.

2) Plan what you want to eat and drink for the evening process. Anything goes. Pick out whatever you want. In the past, for me, it could have been chips and dip, martini, shrimp cocktail, Chunky Monkey ice cream, sushi, chai tea, red wine, sweet potato fries, beef stew . . . whatever sounded good and nurturing on that day.

3) Pick out the music you want to listen to for the closing out process. What music will lift your heart and soul, bring you joy, provide you peace of mind? Maybe it's an eclectic mix of music that will stimulate your creativity.

4) Create the space and environment for writing, reflection and creativity. Oftentimes, it's a fire in the fireplace or a comfy chair with food and drink easily at hand.

Steps 1 - 4 are all about self-nurturing. Taking care of yourself in ways that support you and are meaningful to you. Some of you may be thinking, "I could never do that. My house is too hectic or chaotic." Or, "My family would freak out." All the more reason to create the time and space for yourself, even if it means going away to a retreat center, friend's house, a nook at the library or checking into a boutique hotel for your own R & R.

Regardless of whether you choose to make a day of it or not, it's important to create the time and environment that is conducive to reflection and creativity.

The tools and resources you will need to have available are:

- A blank LifeWheel. A sample can be found in the appendix.
- Your calendars—both work and personal from the past year.
- Blank paper or laptop to record reflections and action plans. My recommendation is to write longhand, rather than using the computer. The act of writing longhand engages the brain in a way that stimulates more creative thinking and innovation.

Step One: Reflection and Renewal—Labeling the Pie

The LifeWheel is a tool to take a snapshot of your life at a given point in time. Start by writing the date at the top of the chart.

On the outside rim of the circle, label each section of the pie with an area of your life. There is a list of possible areas as examples, and you can add others that fit your life and lifestyle. If you need more than the number of sections, just divide a slice to create another piece of the pie.

Step Two: Reflection and Renewal—Rate Your Satisfaction

The next step is to do a quick, gut reaction to your level of satisfaction with each area of your life. Place a dot inside the slice of the pie that reflects your overall feeling about that area of your life. A dot close to the center would indicate a low level of satisfaction, and a dot closer to the rim would indicate a high level of satisfaction.

Do this for each area of your life. Connect the dots so you can see how your life looks at this point in time.

NOTE: It's important that if you had made a conscious decision not to focus on an aspect of your life that you not give it a low rating. For example, if work or family commitments prevented you from regular exercise for a period of time during the year, and you made a conscious decision to place your energy and time in those activities rather than the gym, do not rate your level of satisfaction for your health and wellness as low because that was a deliberate choice.

Step Three: Reflection and Renewal—Self-Acknowledgement

During this step of the process, you will be "closing out the year" by reviewing your calendar to identify things that you did to support yourself, how you took care of yourself, your life, your work and family.

On your blank paper, write one area of your life, such as "health and wellness." When you review your calendars, notice and write down the things that you did to support a healthy lifestyle. List a minimum of three to five things or as many as you can. Only write things that are supportive. Nothing is too elementary or simple. For example: "Had my teeth cleaned two times this year. Had my annual physical, blood work and routine exams. Increased my exercise routine or frequency " While these may not seem worthy of praise to some people, they are, in fact, significant because you made the choice and took the time to take care of yourself.

So often we tend to notice all the things we didn't do or do as much as we hoped to do. This is not the time for those thoughts. Even for the areas that seem somewhat less than what you'd like, write as many positive and supportive statements as you can. Let's say you had a major falling out with a friend during the year that caused you to reevaluate your friendship. One way to write a positive statement would be, "I was more discerning about the people I want to be friends with." Or, "I developed new friendships with people who are aligned with my goals and views of life and what's important to me."

Write three to five or as many statements as you can for each area of your life.

The reason I recommend using your calendars for this process is that our memories can deceive us. Our calendars and our checkbooks or credit card statements will always tell us what's important to us because they're a reflection of how we spend our time and money. We may say one thing, but those are three surefire examples that will tell the truth about how we live our lives.

This is the time to pat yourself on the back and acknowledge yourself for all that you do, all of who you are for other people, all of the ways you contribute to your community and how you support yourself in the complexity of your life.

Take the time to reflect on these things. Bask in the self-acknowledgement and be proud of yourself.

I have been doing this exercise every year for almost 20 years, so I have a stack of LifeWheels and reflections for each year and can see how my life has ebbed and flowed over time. How some areas of my life were stellar and some were dismal. The year 2002 was a dismal year. I have since dramatically and pitifully named the year, "My Year of Quiet Despair." Nothing went right that year or so it seemed. The points on my LifeWheel hovered near the center of the spokes. I had had a series of health issues, and while nothing was life threatening, I was required to have physical therapy for most of the year for various problems. I had had a whirlwind romance that left me broken-hearted, and my two-year-old business was suffering from the fallout of September 11, 2001 and money and jobs were scarce.

When it came time to do my LifeWheel for 2002, I wrote: "I survived 2002." And I did my best to find three or more empowering and supportive statements for each area of my life. It was a good lesson in searching for the bright side of what appeared to be pretty bleak.

Ironically, reflecting back now, some of my best life's lessons about dealing with change came during that period, as well as some of my funniest stories for my keynotes and presentations. Although, admittedly, they weren't very funny when I was in the middle of the muck and drama.

If you take the time to do this exercise each year, you will have a chronicle of your life from a very unique perspective. You will be able to truly reflect on your accomplishments both personal and professional.

Chapter 21

Creating the Future

Now that you have closed out the year, it's time to prepare for the future.

Rather than create New Year's resolutions, which most people forget about a week later, we're going to use a Type T mindset to create *intentions*.

An intention is broader and less specific than a goal. It's more fluid and, yet, directional, without being restrictive like a specific goal.

There are times that specific and measurable goals are essential. And we've all heard about SMART goals—Specific, Measurable, Achievable, Realistic and have a Time Frame. But this is not the time for SMART goals. The point of this part of the process is to create more of a vision of what you want. The intention or vision is about creating a future state that will guide you and help you make choices along the way. Here is an example to help you distinguish the difference between an intention and a goal:

Intention: I intend to make better food choices this year. I will eat fewer processed foods, fewer carbohydrates, more whole foods including fresh vegetables and fruits.

Goal: I will lose 10 pounds by March 1.

Intention: I intend to consciously empower my team and encourage collaboration in all relationships.

Goal: I will set up focus groups to address issues.

While goals are very helpful and provide the action steps needed to achieve specific results, an intention is more about shifting old patterns and creating a new way of life. It's less dramatic and more long term. A goal may provide a mindset of success or failure. You make the goal or you don't. This mindset will not support you in your professional, personal or spiritual growth.

An intention is like having a beacon that shines a light for you to make choices, as you navigate through day-to-day life and work.

When shifting who you are now and transforming your life, it is a slower internal process, and you can't force transformation. Intentions help you in that process.

The next step is to pick three areas of your life to focus on during the upcoming year. It's important to only pick three because three areas for intentionality are manageable. More than three may become like a to-do list, which then becomes a chore and a have-to and no longer serves the purpose of supporting you in your transformation or personal and professional growth.

Some people wonder how to pick the top three areas for focus. My recommendation regarding how to select the areas for focus is to consider what will bring you the most joy in the next year. Think about next year at this time. What would you like to have happened? How do you want to feel next year about this area of your life? Maybe this year was really good, and you want to raise the bar in new ways. Maybe this past year was less than what you wanted, and you want more joy or fulfillment next year.

The point is that creating intentions is not about placing pressure or defined expectations. Intentions are about adding value and joy to your life and the lives of people around you. Because when you are feeling joy and fulfillment and are living authentically, everyone benefits.

We have talked about creating your vision before in other chapters. This final chapter is the culmination or pinnacle of how to enhance, create depth and manifest authentic, transformational leadership in your life and in your work.

Go back and review the key words you chose for yourself. How are they represented in your intentions? Have your intentions come alive through each and every one of your senses? Think not only about your work and personal life. Include your home and work environments. Include your hobbies, passions and interests. This is about creating a vibrant life. A life of vitality that flows effortlessly.

- What will it look like?
- What will you be seeing?
- How will people be responding to you?
- What will you be hearing?
- How will you be listening to others?
- How will you be listening to yourself?
- What will you be feeling?
- How are your vibes aligned with what you want?
- What will you be tasting?
- What smells will be present?
- What vibrational energy will you be bringing to your inter-actions with others?
- What vibrational energy will you be bringing forth into the world?

Some people like to create vision boards of their future life, as a visual reminder of all that is possible. Collect magazines with different subject matter. Scour them for pictures that make you happy and visually support your future vision. Some like to have words on their vision boards. I prefer just having picture. But make it your own and something that you love to look at.

Remember: What you think about and what you focus on is what you get. Are you focused on what you want? Does it make you happy?

Chapter 22

Be the Change

Now is the time to be intentional about your life.

The world, your world, needs you to be awake, alert and alive.

The world, your world, needs you to take action that is aligned with your authentic self.

The world will be a better place if one person at a time aligns and leads with the greatest good in mind.

You always knew you were a leader. That's why you're reading this book. This book and the processes described are for you to define what your transformational leadership style is, so that you can have the greatest impact and have the greatest sense of fulfillment.

It's designed for you to have the hope, trust and conviction that you make a difference. It's for you to have the courage to take action.

Once you do, there's no turning back.

So how does one go about practicing the famous quote by Rabbi Hillel, who lived during the time of Herod the Great, and made popular in a speech by Ronald Reagan in 1981?

If not us, who? If not now, when?

It starts with the realization that it's up to you. It starts with your willingness to be the role model of change. It starts with you being willing to be of service, to make a difference in the lives of those around you, in the workplace and in your communities.

Be willing.

Be willing to be the change.

Be willing to listen. Listen naively, as though you're hearing things for the first time. Be willing to ask questions and not make assumptions.

Be willing to find common ground and learn about other people's goals and dreams and desires.

Create space for trust in communication, so that people feel truly heard and can trust you with their minds and hearts.

Give up the idea that you have to tell, explain or justify your ideas.

Ask permission to share your ideas. Ask permission to see if they are interested in or willing to explore mutually beneficial options.

Be intentional with your thoughts, words and actions.

Be intentional with your vibrational energy, intentional with the "emotions behind your thoughts." When you come from a mindset of service or making a difference or a mindset of collaboration, people will sense that. They may not be able to articulate how they feel about the conversation, but they will feel safe and open with you.

The more you model collaboration, the more everyone one around you will change. They will see you taking ownership of situations and circumstances in a whole new way, so how they respond to you will be different. Old patterns will start to dissolve.

There will be a lightness, a sense of joy and a sense of calm and peace of mind.

Are you willing to give it a try?

Just as we started with the Two Week Challenge of taking ownership of your thoughts, words and action and not blaming and making excuses, we are raising the bar, yet again, as a Type T, authentic leader.

Are you willing to take a new Two Week Challenge modeling purposeful living and Type T leadership in all areas of your life? Perhaps you can start with one or two of your communities, such as family or work colleagues, to test the waters.

What do you have to lose?

What do you have to gain?

Write it down—now.

If not us, who? If not now, when?

The world, your world, needs you to be awake, alert and alive.

The world, your world, needs you to take action that is aligned with your authentic self.

The world will be a better place when you're aligned and lead with the greatest good in mind.

I wish you love, joy and peace of mind as you live intentionally and authentically, making a difference in the world around you.

Be the change.

Marty Stanley

Appendix—Flying Solo

Some people may find that being a solo entrepreneur is the route they want to take to express their skills, talents and to make a greater contribution. As mentioned in Chapter 7, starting your own business after a career in an organizational setting is not for the faint of heart. It requires stamina, persistence and, most of all, commitment to your own vision for the future.

The Reality of Being on Your Own

I have several colleagues who were downsized from large corporations and were bitten by the entrepreneurial bug. After all, it is the American Dream, isn't it? To have your own business? To create your own destiny?

I read many years ago that only 1 in 100 people are financially successful and satisfied when they leave a corporate environment to start their own business. I am fortunate to be that one in one hundred. There were many lean years, but I was always able to pay my bills. It was humbling and horrifying to watch so many people struggle and, for many, to lose significant savings, 401k accounts, homes and even marriages. Many didn't know when to stop working on that dream and start redefining something more in alignment with what they know and do best—and have a sustainable income.

Unfortunately, many people who started their own businesses after leaving a corporate job were unrealistic about what it really takes and the amount of energy required. For example, most underestimated the impact that when you're on your own, there's no "help desk" to fix your computer or accounting department to set up your record-keeping systems, no marketing department to create brochures, websites and other marketing pieces and no sales department to sell your products or services.

You are the CEO, CFO, CMO, COO and chief cook and bottle washer. Some of the smartest people I knew in the corporate world made really awful decisions, trusting the information they had available and made bad financial decisions that hit the bottom line immediately. There is no safety net.

I certainly have had my share of poor financial decisions and unsatisfactory vendor relationships. Being on your own requires a tremendous amount of energy to stay focused and intentional about fulfilling your purpose through your own business. The highs are high, and the lows are low. And, in the early days of being on your own, it's very easy to get caught up in the emotions of both ends of the spectrum. It can be challenging to stay balanced. But if you don't, you will burn out and drive everyone crazy, especially yourself. Being a sole proprietor or having your own business isn't for everyone. There is a lot at risk, financially and emotionally.

Following Your Bliss

There's a lot of hype that says, "Follow your bliss and the money will follow." At the risk of sounding like "Debbie Downer," that's not always true. You still have to have a good business concept, a business plan and action plans to help you reach your goals. Good intentions aren't enough.

Woe to the entrepreneur who follows the "bliss business plan."

Your thoughts, words AND ACTIONS must be aligned.

Feasibility Study

Many universities and community colleges have courses to help you conduct a feasibility study to see if your concept is viable. This is particularly helpful when you are creating a business based on a new concept or a product/service that is not currently readily available.

Another option is the Kauffman FastTrac program http://fasttrac. org/, which is the program I used when starting my life coaching business. Kauffman FastTrac is a global provider of education courses that equip aspiring and existing entrepreneurs with the business skills and insights, tools, resources, and networks to start and grow successful businesses.

I had heard that more than 80% of the participants did *not* start their business after participating in a business feasibility program. Some might think of this as failure. But consider the amount of money and time that would have been lost due to a poor concept or plan.

Family and Financial Matters

Another consideration is the level of support from immediate family members. If your spouse or partner has a high need for stability and security, this needs to be a major consideration. There is no stability or security when starting your own business. It's important to have in-depth discussions about the opportunities and ramifications of being on you own.

Talk to your financial planner before making any business decisions. My opinion is that you should count on having a minimum of one year's expenses in reserve. Remember, you probably won't have health insurance coverage, and there are a lot of start up costs, depending on your business.

One Foot In/One Foot Out

Some people try to straddle the entrepreneurial tightrope by saying they'll keep their day job and do this on the side. This may work, depending on the nature of the business. If it's a tangible product, this may be possible. If it's a professional service, such as consulting, it's a fine line to success. Many hang out their shingle as a consultant or coach, only to jump ship when a job offer comes along. Again, being on your own is not for everyone and being an independent consultant can be tough.

Networking

When people leave an organizational setting and start their own business, many are surprised to learn that you have to "earn your stripes" all over again. I've had clients who have said, "I've worked 40 years and want to do something new… but I don't want to work that hard." Well, when you start something new, you often have to establish yourself as an expert in a new arena. And that takes work—sometimes hard work.

It's important to talk to people who have made the transition from organizational contributor to solo entrepreneur. If they are in a similar field or area of work, all the better. If they see you as competition or are reluctant to help, just know they're still a Type A leader and learn what you can but don't take it personally.

There are a plethora of networking opportunities and everyone will have ideas on a group to join or become a member or new circles of people to meet. This can be one of the hardest areas to manage because you never know who you'll meet and what information they might have that can assist you as you navigate this new world.

It will take time to establish trusted business relationships that, in turn, will lead to paying customers or clients. Use your best judgment when allocating your time and resources to networking opportunities. It can be great fun and exciting to share your ideas and visions for the future, just make sure it's balanced and productive.

There are a myriad of other considerations and things to do if you decide that flying solo is for you. Hopefully this brief description will give you some ideas about what to expect and some considerations that will help you decide if it's right for you.

Worksheet: Solo Entrepreneur or Not

Type T leaders often want to make a change in career that is a better fit for their vision for the future.

Purpose: To do a preliminary assessment as to whether it's best to go solo or find a different work environment.

What to do: Reflect on environments that are best suited for you or how best to use your strengths.

A Different Organization

1) The work environments that I like best are:

Size (revenue or number of employees):

Industry:

Location (city, rural, global):

Not for profit:

2) The type of culture that I like best is:

Structured, with established policies and procedures.

Traditional management style.

Entrepreneurial/start-up.

Entrepreneurial/growing and established.

3) The skills I want to contribute most are:

4) I need to update or learn the following skills to be more prepared and qualified for the work that I want in the future:

5) I'll know another organization is a good fit when:

I'm ready to go solo:

1) I have 12 - 18 months of financial reserves to cover all expenses, and I understand the risks involved.

2) I have a business plan or am willing to do a business plan to determine the feasibility of my own business.

3) My family and other significant people in my life agree with this decision.

4) I have the emotional and physical stamina and support to be an entrepreneur.

5) To be successful in this endeavor, I need to:

Exercises

Chapter 2—Foundational Tools for Transformation

Two Week Challenge

Purpose: To objectively determine and assess the frequency and nature of what you think and talk about. To reduce the amount of time focused on negative experiences that happened in the past.

What to do: For two weeks, listen to and observe your thoughts and internal chatter and the topics you talk about with others.

The things that I think or talk about repeatedly are:

These things happened: Days ago. Weeks ago. Years ago. Decades ago.

When I think about them, I feel:

I know I can't change what happened, but I can limit the amount of time I think or speak about them. When I notice myself thinking negatively for 17 seconds or more, I will think about things that make me happy or make me laugh. Two positive thoughts that I will do to change this pattern are:

Chapter 3—Transformation From the Inside Out

Healthy Body, Mind and Spirit

Purpose: Type T leaders understand the importance of taking care of their body, mind and spirit. They also know changes don't happen overnight and that shifting to a healthy lifestyle is a process and a long-term commitment.

What to do: Identify the changes you'd like to make in the next 90 days and what you're committed to doing on an ongoing basis.

Food and beverage choices:

I will eat/drink more of:

I will eat less of:

Exercise/movement:

I will continue or try:

I want to continue or look into the following spiritual practices to support me on this journey:

Changes I want to make regarding what I read and watch on television are:

I want to look into the following groups and/or educational or networking opportunities to support me on my journey:

Hobbies or entertainment I want to continue or add to my life are:

Other changes:

Chapter 4—Type T Means Getting Out of B.E.D.

Two Week Challenge for Getting Out of B.E.D.

Purpose: To objectively determine and assess the frequency that you blame others, make excuses or are in denial—both verbally and in your thoughts. To minimize the frequency and amount of time that you place yourself in the "victim" role.

What to do: For two weeks, listen to and observe your thoughts, internal chatter and how you may blame or makes excuses when talking to others.

I've learned that I have a tendency to:

To shift this pattern, I will ask myself: What can I say or do to change this situation or circumstance?

Here's what I'll say instead:

Financial Integrity

Type T Leaders have financial integrity. They take ownership, accountability and responsibility for their financial choices, including managing debt, saving for the future and paying taxes.

I plan to improve my financial integrity by:

Chapter 5—Creating Intentions and Alignment

Type T Leaders are intentional about who they are and what they want to contribute to their communities.

Creating Intentions

Purpose: To start the process or refine your thinking about what you want for your future and how you want to contribute to your communities.

What to do: Think about your communities and who you want to be, what you want to be known for and/or how you want contribute.

These are my current communities and how I want to contribute to them and/or how I want to be known by them:

1.

2.

3.

4.

Knowing What I Want

This T-chart will help me identify my intentions and gain clarity:

Things I Don't Want   The Opposite of That Is

To align my thoughts, words and actions with my intentions, I want to:

Chapter 6—Closing the Past and Creating the New You

Closing Out the Past

Purpose: To close out the past, it's important to know what you *don't want* to repeat and why.

What to do: Create a T-chart list of what you don't want to repeat and why.

Things I don't want, don't like or don't want to settle for:	How I feel about those things:

What I have learned that will help me move forward in a positive way:

Creating the Future

Purpose: Start the process of identifying what you do want for the future.

What to do: Look at the examples listed in the previous exercise and write whatever might be the *opposite*. What are the emotions you want to feel in the future? This T-chart will help you gain clarity.

What I want: How I will feel or want to feel:

My Key Words

Purpose: To identify the specific words that you want to be known for. These words will be your guide for all communication, decisions and choices. Think of them as your own personal "core values."

What to do: List as many words as you can. There are examples in Chapter 6. Then, identify the top five to seven words that really resonate for you.

Putting the Key Words Into Action

Purpose: Type T leaders are intentional and deliberate in how they communicate and in the choices they make. Your Key Words will support you in your journey to being a Type T leader.

What to do: When faced with challenging situations or circumstances that would normally elicit a negative response, ask yourself the following questions by inserting one or more of your key words:

What would I be saying if I were being . . .

What would I be doing if I were being …

What would I be thinking if I were being …

How would I be feeling if I were being …

What would I be hearing if I were being…

How would others feel when they are around me if I were being …

What would others be seeing or hearing if I were being …

Chapter 7—The New Normal

Things have changed dramatically since 2008, including new technologies, demographics, regulations and societal norms. Type T leaders recognize that there are multiple changes that have taken place, if not personally, certainly at work or among their friends and family.

Purpose: To acknowledge how many things have changed in a short period of time, the impact of these changes and determine if you're keeping up with the changes.

What to do: Identify the changes at work and on a personal level and what you're doing differently as a result of these changes.

Changes at work since 2008:

Changes in technology at work include:

Changes in regulations include:

Changes in workforce or customer demographics include:

Other changes:

Changes at home and personally since 2008:

Changes in my health or health of my family include:

My lifestyle has changed by:

My friends, family and social activities have changed by:

Other changes:

Chapter 9—Unraveling the Myths and Mysteries of Power

Type T leaders understand power and how to use it effectively.

Perceptions of Power

Purpose: To assess your perceptions of power.

What to do: Reflect on your perceptions of power and how they influence you.

1. My current perceptions of power are:

2. The people who come to mind who use power effectively are:

3. I've known people who abused power by:

4. When others exercise power *over me*, I feel:

5. Just the thought of having power makes me feel:

Using Power Positively

Purpose: To identify ways that you currently use or could use your power positively in the future.

What to do: Think about how you can empower others.

1. I empower my team by sharing the vision and goals of the department or organization and how they fit in and can contribute.

2. I ask for input from team members for ways to contribute to the department, organizational vision or goals.

3. I provide accurate and timely expectations and feedback by:

4. I hold individuals and team members accountable by:

5. Other:

Chapter 10—Giving Up Fear, Old Patterns and the Need to Be Right

Type T leaders strive for collaboration and are willing to give up old communication patterns that are not empowering and they are more concerned about doing what is right rather than being right.

Giving Up Old Patterns

Purpose: To recognize and acknowledge your personal unproductive or disempowering communication patterns and the impact on results.

What to do: Identify ways that you communicate out of fear and create new, empowering ways to express yourself.

1. There are times I try to control outcomes by:

2. Sometimes I manipulate or try to dominate others to do what I want by:

3. Sometimes I withhold my thoughts or opinions to control a situation because:

4. What fear is driving this approach?

5. What would happen if I didn't try to control or force an outcome?

6. How important is it for me to be right?

7. What do I need to give up?

Chapter 17—The Power of Courageous Collaboration

Type T leaders strive to demonstrate a collaborative spirit.

Purpose: To create an inclusive and empowering culture through collaborative communication that is consistent with the vision and goals of the organization.

What to do: Find ways to demonstrate collaboration at work, home and in your communities. What would some of these be?

1.   What would I be saying if I were being collaborative? At work? At home? In my community?

2.   What would I be doing if I were acting in a more collaborative manner? At work? At home? In my community?

3. What would my organization, community or family look and sound like if we were acting with each other's best interests at heart?

4. What would we be doing if we were looking out for the good of the whole?

5. Most importantly, what difference would this make to our quality of life?

Chapter 20—Planning for Success

Two life wheels are provided for you—one as a sample and a blank one for you to use as part of the process of closing out your year.

SAMPLE LIFE WHEEL
How well do you get around?

DIRECTIONS:

1. Label each section with what's important or essential to having the life you love. Examples could be:

Friends & Family	Growth & Development	Spiritual Alignment
Health	Financial Prosperity	Romance & Intimacy
Career	Fun & Recreation	Hobbies
Art & Music	Community Involvement	Physical Environment

2. Seeing the center of the wheel as zero and the outer edge as 10, rank your level of satisfaction with each area of your life by drawing a line, creating a new outer edge.

3. The new perimeter of the circle represents Your Life Wheel. Imagine how bumpy the ride might be if this were a real wheel.

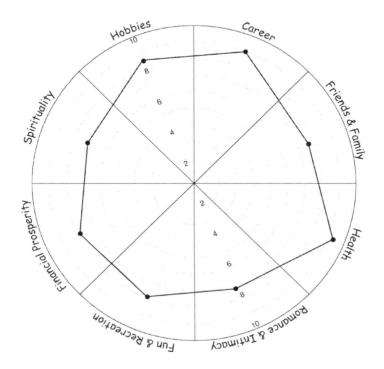

YOUR LIFE WHEEL
How well do you get around?

DIRECTIONS:

1. Label each section with what's important or essential to having the life you love. Examples could be:

Friends & Family	*Growth & Development*	*Spiritual Alignment*
Health	*Financial Prosperity*	*Romance & Intimacy*
Career	*Fun & Recreation*	*Hobbies*
Art & Music	*Community Involvement*	*Physical Environment*

2. Seeing the center of the wheel as zero and the outer edge as 10, rank your level of satisfaction with each area of your life by drawing a line, creating a new outer edge.

3. The new perimeter of the circle represents Your Life Wheel. Imagine how bumpy the ride might be if this were a real wheel.

Take a look at the example of a completed life wheel. Complete the directions for the life wheel based on how you see your life *right now*. Put the date at the top of the page.

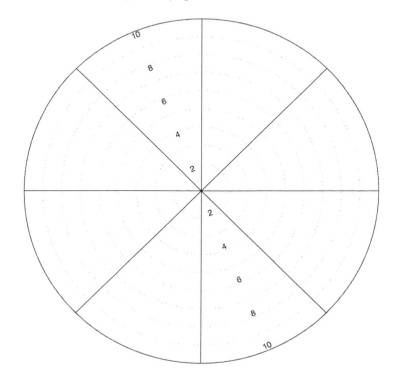

Suggested Reading List

Highly recommended

Relationships

* *The Five Love Languages*—Gary Chapman

The Love You Deserve—Scott Peck

Self-esteem/Life Purpose

You Can Heal Your Life—Louise Hay

Take Time For Your Life—Cheryl Richardson

The Purpose of Your Life—Cheryl Richardson

Unlimited Power—Anthony Robbins

The Power of Purpose—James Lieder

Business/Leadership

Strengths Finders 2.0—Tom Rath

Good to Great—Jim Collins

Real Power – Business Lessons of the Tao Te Ching—James Autry and Stephen Mitchell

*Real Power -Stages of Personal Power in Organizations—Janet O. Hagberg

*Rich Dad, Poor Dad—Robert Kiyosaki

Enlightened Leadership—Ed Oakley and Doug Krug

Leading From the Heart—Choosing Courage Over Fear In The Workplace – Kay Gilley

The Tao of Leadership— John Heider

Health and Wellness

The 10 Day Sugar Detox—Mark Hyman, M.D.

If The Buddha Came to Dinner—Hale Sophia Schatz

Transformational/Spiritual

*The Four Agreements—Don Miguel Ruiz

*The Power of Intention—Dr. Wayne Dyer

*Excuse Me Your Life Is Waiting—Lynn Grabhorn

*A Year of Living Consciously—Gay Hendricks

The Mastery of Love—Don Miguel Ruiz

Loving What Is—Byron Katie

How to Use Your Twelve Gifts From God—William Warch

The Power of Now—Eckhart Tolle

Conversations With God—Neale Donald Walsh

Anatomy of the Spirit—Caroline Myss

Soul Life —Thomas Moore

Real Magic—Wayne Dyer

Manifest Your Destiny—Wayne Dyer

Divine Intuition—Lynn Robinson

Ask and You Shall Receive—Esther Hicks

Spiritual Economics—Eric Butterworth

Science Related

From Chaos To Coherence—Doc Childre and Bruce Cryer

Leadership and the New Science—Margaret Wheatley

Power vs. Force—David R. Hawkins

Author Biography

MARTY STANLEY knows about change and transformation. After several minimum wage jobs, she earned her college degree leading to a 20 year career in the corporate world. As a human resource executive, she led initiatives to meet changing conditions at multiple, diverse companies, up to and including international and billion dollar businesses. Then, 15 years ago, Marty transformed herself again, becoming a highly successful solo entrepreneur with her company, Dynamic Dialog, Inc., as a national speaker, author and consultant on personal and organizational change. Marty continues to help others create change and alter their outcomes through transformational leadership and its focus on empowerment, collaboration and sustainability.

Printed in the United States
By Bookmasters